30 DAYS *to* FINDING *and* KEEPING SASSY SIDEKICKS *and* BFFs

30 Days
to
FINDING
and
KEEPING
SASSY
SIDEKICKS
and **BFFs**

a friendship field guide by
CLEA HANTMAN

Delacorte Press

Published by Delacorte Press, an imprint of Random House Children's Books, a division of Random House, Inc., New York • Copyright © 2009 by Clea Hantman • All rights reserved. • Delacorte Press and colophon are registered trademarks of Random House, Inc. • Visit us on the Web! www.randomhouse.com/teens • Educators and librarians, for a variety of teaching tools, visit us at www.randomhouse.com/teachers • *Library of Congress Cataloging-in-Publication Data* • Hantman, Clea. • 30 days to finding and keeping sassy sidekicks and BFFs : a friendship manual / Clea Hantman . — 1st trade pbk. ed. • p. cm. • ISBN 978-0-385-73623-7 (tr. pbk.) • 1. Friendship. I. Title. II. Title: Thirty days to finding and keeping sassy sidekicks and BFFs. • BF575.F66H37 2009 • 158.2'5—dc22 • 2007051599 • Printed in the United States of America • 10 9 8 7 6 5 4 3 2 1 • First Trade Paperback Edition • Random House Children's Books supports the First Amendment and celebrates the right to read.

I didn't fully understand the depth and beauty of girl

friendship until I met Keva, Karen, Michelle, Amy and the

rest of the PS gang. So I am forever grateful to them for their

sass, strength, support, smarts and straight-up fun.

But this book is really for all my young friends, and I want to

name just a few: Loren, Haley, Macky, Rachel and Mara; and

of course I can't forget Natalie, Sonya, Greta, Izzy, Emmy,

Michaela, Zoe and last but never, ever least: Tuesday.

xoxoxo

contents

HOW TO OVERCOME THE HARD TIMES: THE OBSTACLES

HOW TO ACHIEVE THAT SECOND "F" IN "BFF": THE FOREVER FRIEND

INTRODUCTION

You know what is shocking to me? All those magazines we read, they cover makeup and hair, hot sexy boys and quizzes, but they don't talk about friendship—it's as if it's assumed that all is perfect in friend-land. But is it? I mean, always? Because frankly, a friendship is a relationship, and relationships are hard and ever-changing and need to be worked at time and time again.

If you don't have a BFF right here, right now, that's okay. This book can help you steer clear of the bad ones, attract the good ones and guide you to treating them well so that they stick around. If you do have one, this here book will only make things brighter and better and help you get over the inevitable hurdles.

The following is a statement that should not have to be made, and yet it does: *Other girls are not the enemy.* They aren't your competition, despite what some CW shows would have you believe. Girls should be seen as our team-mates, with us through thick and thin, by our side cheering us on, not antagonizing us. I am hereby encouraging you to look at other, unknown girls not as adversaries or rivals but as potential friends.

Because if we nurture them and make the effort, our girlfriend-ships can last a lifetime. Girlfriends can be the most meaningful people in our worlds. They can be some of the most rewarding parts of our lives. And they tend to stick around longer than boyfriends. I challenge you to make the effort and celebrate your friendships, solidifying the place deep in your soul for your greatest girlfriends. But how?

Well, you can't pick your family members. But you can pick your friends (and your nose). So do so, wisely. (The friends, not the nose.)

The ultimate way to be happy and live well is to be surrounded by good friends. They make strawberries sweeter, a movie funnier and a day at the beach even more enjoyable. Great friends should inspire you, spur you on and share your experiences. Have you ever noticed that when you study with people who really *get* the material, you understand it better? The same goes for friends. When you are with people who are good at being friends, you become a better friend. Lousy friends drag you down, drain your soul, wear you out. You have the ability to choose which sorts you surround yourself with.

These choices make up our world and our experiences. You have the power to make good choices; you just need to be informed. What are you looking for in a friend? What means the most to you? What won't you put up with? What shouldn't you put up with? These questions and more will be answered in the next thirty days.

I don't come to you as a registered or licensed expert. I come to you as someone who has screwed up my share of friendships and made a couple of messes, but who has emerged on the other side with a small yet sturdy boatload of terrific gal pals. It can be rough sailing at times, and that's how I know firsthand that it all takes great care and concern and effort. And I also know it's worth every bit of that hard work.

I've divided this book into four sections. The first will cover the basics of friendship, what it is and how to make it happen. The second takes it to another level, giving you ideas about how to make the bond bondier. (Not a word? Tough.) The third section covers the major pitfalls and obstacles of friendship today and how to overcome or at least deal with those. And finally, the fourth and last chapter steers the friendship up, up, up to the highest pinnacle of goodness, elevating it to Mount Everest height. Each section is split into days, with thirty in all. And every day I provide you with a concept to think about, as well as an activity to do. And because I believe music magnifies our feelings and self-discoveries, I've suggested a song that I think illustrates the concept for each day.

Now let's get to work.

HOW TO MAKE AND KEEP FRIENDS: THE FRIENDSHIP BASICS

Methinks there needs to be an Intro to Friendship class at every high school on what it means to be a friend. But since I don't know of a single school that has one, that's where I'm going to start. Before you skip this section because you think it's beneath you or not applicable to your life, let me beg you to reconsider.

Sometimes even the bestest friends in the world need a refresher on what it takes to be a world-class pal. Heck, I need one regularly and I'm writing this book. Friendship may seem basic and obvious to you now, but when you dissect it like that poor frog in biology, you'll see there is so much more to it than you first thought.

If you flat-out need to make new friends, this is of course *exactly* where to start. Know that you're not alone. Due to various circumstances such as a new school or job, old friends moving on and drifting apart or a plain ol' lack of the finer points of basic social skills, many, many girls are looking to start fresh on the friendship train. So with that said, all aboard . . . *toot, toot.*

Day One
ANTHROPOPHOBIA!
(AKA THE FEAR OF PEOPLE!)

Being Open to New People vs.
Being a Loner

New people scare me.
My room is safer, okay?
But boy, am I bored.

Want more friends? Want better friends? Of course you do, that's why you have this bright little book in your hands. If you can't be open to meeting new people, you can't achieve your goals of bigger, better friendships. So this is the A–number one lesson right here.

Don't get me wrong, being a loner has its perks: it's easier than making friends. You can be lazy and be a loner, because being in a friendship does take effort. And if you're a loner you don't have to waste any time on the phone, or out in the sunshine frolicking with others, or having meaningful face-to-face conversations with possible confidants. As a loner, you can be completely self-obsessed and all about you, you, you. See, perks.

That was sarcasm, in case it's lost on the page. Life is hard without friends. And not nearly as much fun.

Now, being open to new people, as I said, can take a little work. You have to ask questions. You have to pay attention to other people, you have to listen, you have to look them in the eye. This is hard stuff, right?

Not exactly.

Do you like to talk about yourself? I do. I even talk to myself by myself about myself. I know what you're thinking right about now: "She is loony." But everyone, for the most part, enjoys talking about themselves. Which is exactly how you get new people to talk to you.

You ask them about themselves.

For example, say you have spotted a new person somewhere—school, work, a class or club. You think, "She looks nice," or cool, or whatever. So you approach her and you ask her a question. You could even start with a compliment and then follow up with a question.

- "I love your bag—did you make that yourself?"
- "You have awesome hair—who cuts it?"
- "Haven't seen you here before—where are you from?"

See? Not so hard.

But here's the tricky part: you have to actually listen to what they say! This is where I used to go south—I would check out and think about other things, like I'd be trying to read her body language to see if she was receptive to having a conversation, or I'd be thinking about a new question rather than actually listening to her answers, which—

duh!—(a) would let me know if she was interested in talking to me *and* (b) would provide me with a lead-in to another question.

So to recap, the first step to making friends is to ask questions and then listen for the answer. You already know how to do this; you learned back in grade school. We all just need a little reminding sometimes.

> ### And Another Thing . . .
> Even if you're thinking, "Hey, I'm just here to make the friendships I've got stronger, I don't need to meet new people," well, you're wrong. Because bet you five bucks situations will arise (new college, new job, new town) when you will be meeting new people, and wouldn't it be great if you were armed and ready to greet them with friendship from the get-go?

ACTIVITY 1

There is one more component to this "Meeting New People" exercise. You have to hear, use and remember their names. And don't even try telling yourself, "Oh, I'm not good at names, I have a bad memory," because that is *phooey*. Remembering people's names is not a skill you are born with, like the ability to curl your tongue. It's something you have to work at. And here's how:

The best way to get someone to tell you her name is to introduce yourself. "Hi, I'm Clea Hantman." Ninety-nine times out of a hundred, the other person will then say, "Hello, I'm _____." Right? If you don't hear the name clearly, or the other person said it fast, or it's unusual (like mine), feel free to ask her to repeat it—that shows you care enough to get it right. You can say "Pardon?" Or "What was that again?" Or ask her to spell it for you, and as she does, visualize the letters across her forehead.

And now here comes the work—it's a four-step process that I think will help you remember names:

LOOK (at her face)
LISTEN (to her name)
PICTURE an exaggerated, silly image of her in your head
REPEAT!

Let's start with the look. Look at the person's face for a moment and try to find a particular quality that stands out—is it her eyebrows? Her eyes? Her ears? Her face shape?

Listen to her name; then say the name again to yourself in your head.

Then visualize. Can you turn something about the name into a picture? Does it sound like something? Or does it rhyme with something that can be a picture?

Let's take the name Michelle as an example: "Michelle" might make you think of a shell. If Michelle were in front of us, we could ask ourselves if her eyebrows look like shells, or her nose. If so, imagine this Michelle with shells replacing her eyebrows, or her nose. Michelle also makes *me* think of that Beatles song "Michelle," and the next line is "*ma belle.*" So I would think about a bell, and maybe I'd picture Michelle with a big cowbell around her neck. It's these kinds of ridiculous and exaggerated images that we remember. Or perhaps you already know someone named Michelle. So how does this Michelle in front of you look like the Michelle you already know? Or you could imagine them sitting together having a conversation about being named Michelle.

The last step is to repeat the name out loud. Try to say her name two more times in this first conversation. "So, Michelle, where do you buy your yarn for those knitting projects?" and "It was nice meeting you, Michelle."

So what is your activity of the day? To go out there and meet someone new and really, truly learn her name. Use these name tricks today and as often as you can. Can't find any new people to meet today? Try this out on the Starbucks barista or a waiter. Once you get in the habit, it will become second nature. And you'll be meeting new people in no time. Lazy loners be damned!

SONG OF THE DAY:
THE WHITE STRIPES,
"WE'RE GOING TO BE FRIENDS"
When we were younger, it was a bit simpler, wasn't it? Bugs and walks to school and sitting side by side were enough to elicit deep feelings of friendship. This is one of the sweetest, most childlike visions of friendship in song. Share it with a new friend.

DaY TWO
TURN THAT FROWN
UPSIDE DOWN

Smiling vs. Frowning

Kittens and puppies,
Rainbows and unicorn love
Make me gag and hurl.

Don't dismiss the joy of a smile as an empty, fleeting moment or the equivalent of a cute puppy or kitty. A smile can disarm people, put them at ease, brighten your entire face and outfit—geez, it can even make your hair look better. And did you know that it takes fewer muscles to smile than it does to turn it upside down?

A smile is telling. It immediately informs the world that you are a person who enjoys life, makes the best of situations, has a good sense of humor and likes herself.

A smile is power. Slapping one on your face can change your mood and other people's moods—it's hard to be grumpy when the person next to you has a big, broad, welcoming smile. Smiles open doors and make people in high places (teachers, professors, hiring professionals) take notice. People don't remember a good haircut they saw on someone earlier in the day, but they do remember a fabulous smile because there is life behind it.

A smile is a great response. When someone tells you or asks you something and you greet that statement or question with a smile, it can signify to the other person that you are listening (if you are, that is).

A smile is a flaw fixer. When you're feeling low, you probably hunch over a little, hang your head, shuffle your feet. When you put a smile on your face, you can't help holding your chin higher, which in turn straightens out your posture, which leads to less shuffling. No one notices the stain on your shirt or the dog hair on your coat, because they are looking at your face, at your smile.

A smile, if nothing else, shows that you are probably a pleasure to be around. But think about the opposite: the frown. That tells people something too—it tells them you are irritable, grumpy, uninterested in life and in listening to what others have to say. It makes people feel lousy and uncomfortable. It's a terrible response to a question or a statement; it just makes the other person feel like she's wasted her time. And it makes your back seem hunchier and your brows seem heavier and, oddly, even makes your hair seem duller. A frown is a distancer—no one likes to be down in the dumps.

So if you're trying to meet new people and have meaningful connections with others, it seems pretty obvious that a smile is a must-have this season and every other.

ACTIVITY 2

This activity is more like a challenge. For one week, smile. I mean it, smile at everyone, even people you've simply never noticed before—the lady behind the counter at the convenience store, the old dude walking his dog, the person who serves you your lunch, the strangers you see most every day and the ones you don't, kids down the hall, the sullen clerk at the indie music store, the ticket taker at the movies. Smile at them with bright eyes. Smile at the cute boy rather than turning your head away in some weird mix of embarrassment and fear. Smile at the girls who don't smile back. Smile like you mean it. For the whole gosh-darn day.

At the end of the day, come back here and answer these questions:

Whom did you smile at? _____
_____
_____
_____
_____

Did anyone smile back? _____
_____

Did anyone talk to you who might not have otherwise?
_____
_____

How did it feel? _____
_____

Do you think it improved your day at all? _____

_____

_____

I'm confident that you'll be pleasantly surprised by your findings.

SONG OF THE DAY:
THE KILLERS, "SMILE LIKE YOU MEAN IT"
This song is basically saying exactly what I am, only in a sexier, Brandon Flowers New Wave sort of way— you're wasting your time if you're walking through life without putting forth the effort of a real smile. For a more soothing version of this song, check out David Gray's cover.

THE COMMON DENOMINATOR

Shared Interests vs. Nothing in Common

I do not eat meat;
She loves steak—even bacon.
Can we be real friends?

Is it necessary that you and your friends have things in common?

No.

Is it better if you have *everything* in common?

No.

Truth is, you want individuals, people who have their own lives and loves and desires and dreams, as friends. The less you have in common with your friends, the more you can learn from their experiences. You don't want them to have exactly the same dreams or desires as you, right? I mean, I'm strongly against cloning.

But having a thing in common, or a few things in common, can make friendships easier. It gives you activities to do and things to talk about. It can give you a common outlook on a situation. All good things.

And your interests can lead you to new friends.

Even if it appears that you don't have anything in common with a person, you probably still do. Maybe it's something less tangible than a hobby. Maybe it's an outlook on life. An attitude. An opinion. Don't dismiss potential friends because you wear different clothes or do different things. There is great value in being friends with people who are different from you, and chances are, if you have something like an outlook in common with a person, you'll have an even stronger bond with him or her than with the person who likes to knit or play soccer like you do but who views the world from a wildly different perspective.

What I'm getting at is that your friends don't all have to be from the same tribe. When I was younger and in school, there was always a girl or two who could be friends with everyone, people from all the different cliques. And those girls always stood out as the happiest, most joyful people in a sea of sullen teen angst. Think there is a connection? Perhaps their ability to widen their circles beyond just a small group led them to more diversity, more intrigue and, gosh darn it, more fun.

ACTIVITY 3

A great place to find new friends—and strengthen the bond between existing ones—is in a club. Clubs are not just for little kids or ancient bridge-playing ladies. Clubs are cool again, and rightfully so. They allow you to explore a beloved hobby, or an altogether new hobby, with people who are also interested in pursuing said hobby. Fertile friendship ground, if you ask me!

So your exercise today is to join or start a club. And it's easier than ever, what with all the coffee shops around town (great meeting places) and the ease of creating and maintaining a blog online (to attract new members or give the ones you have all the important information).

Here are just a few ideas—start with these or brainstorm your very own:

A CLUB ABOUT COMIC BOOKS, BOOKS OR WRITING
Hold your club meetings at a local bookstore. Pick a book or comic book to read before each meeting. Or if the club is about writing, give an assignment for each member to complete before the next meeting. And remember, you can get specific. This can be a club about manga or chick-lit books or even writing music reviews!

A CLUB ABOUT COOKING, FOOD OR RESTAURANTS
Meet in someone's kitchen each week and cook food from a particular region of the world. Or just desserts. Or have cheap lunches around town together and then review them for a blog. Work together on writing your very own cookbook—you could even try to get it published.

A CLUB ABOUT A CRAFT
These are everywhere—knitting clubs, crocheting clubs, sewing circles, quilting bees—and more than ever, they're

filled with younger people creating craft that is art. If you can't find an existing one, start your own—hit up the local fabric store or yarn shop to host it. Or take it on the road— at a different member's house each week or a different coffee shop each month!

A CLUB ABOUT FASHION, DESIGN AND CLOTHES

Get together to swap sewing patterns, old clothes and ideas and to just plain talk about fashion. Bring stacks of *W* and *Vogue* and *Nylon* and rip out pages that strike you as golden—make collages, scrapbooks, inspirational boards. Help each other spice up your closets and your old-rut routines.

A CLUB ABOUT MOVIES

This one's easy: meet every other week for a different movie and then go for dessert and Frappuccinos afterward to discuss your thoughts, reactions and feelings about what you just saw. Even if you can't all see the movie at the same time and place, you can still get together at a later date and discuss. You can even watch an old movie together at a different member's house once a month. A movie rental and microwave popcorn are practically free and just as much fun!

A CLUB ABOUT BASEBALL

I have this friend Jeudi and she loves everything about baseball—watching it, cheering, getting obnoxious at the game, talking about it all afterward, even eating ballpark food. Think she's alone? No way. If you love baseball, find other girls (and boys) who do too and hit the home games.

For the away ones, congregate at someone's house and make sure to stock up on plenty of snacks.

And of course there are a zillion other interests, including drama, music, painting, horseback riding, science, politics, ballet, photography, skateboarding, cycling, blogging and on and on and on.

Other ideas for clubs: _____

_____

_____

_____

_____

On That Note . . .

You can even make your club about a hobby but take it to another level, like using that hobby to make a difference in other people's lives. A designer friend of a friend of mine named Shaney Jo and her pal Mona took their passion for art and their concern for the lack of breast cancer education and created Keep A Breast. It's a nonprofit organization that makes one-of-a-kind plaster torso casts of women, has artists from all walks of life paint them and then auctions the pieces off, with all proceeds going to research and education. Shaney Jo has now traveled all over the world, made new friends everywhere she's been, cultivated her hobby and raised awareness— and a buncha money, to boot.

Day Four
THE SECRET TO SUCCESS

Kindness vs. Cruelty

Sticks and stones break bones,
Mean words break your heart and mind.
Friendship, kindness heal.

What a basic concept—*kindness*. It's so obvious that it is often just plain overlooked. Kindness is this intense and gargantuan and overwhelming thing, and yet it's obtainable to us all. You don't have to have a boyfriend or even a best friend to feel or give kindness. You can give it to and receive it from the people on the street, your neighbors, your folks and, of course, your friends.

So you're saying to yourself about now, "Yeah, I'm kind." Good. Great. But even I can admit that there are times when I'm not so kind. You know when? When I'm overtired or stressed out, maybe when I haven't had any coffee. Maybe no one was kind to me that morning. And you know that kindness begets kindness. It's one of those pay-it-forward, contagious-yawn things.

When people are unkind (or, taken to the extreme, downright cruel), it can pummel you. It's shocking and disorienting, and while it may not break any bones, it can still send pain reverberating through your body. Do you remember what I said three sentences ago? Kindness is contagious. Unfortunately, so is cruelty. That mean girl who is terrorizing other girls is probably getting her share, directed squarely at her or someone she loves, someplace else. It's so much easier to be cruel and mean and just plain unkind when others around you are doing the same thing. It produces a culture of cruelty. And that is yet another reason to spread kindness around. It discourages the mean and encourages the nice.

Like I said from the get-go, friendships are work, and you've got to put forth some effort. Kindness can take effort—like when you're trying to be kind to that person who is driving you utterly bonkers—but mostly, it's pretty easy. And it's one of the only things in this book that is.

Want to attract more friends? The number-one way is not a new haircut or a magic wand that will make you the most popular gal in town. It's kindness. People notice a girl who smiles and treats people with genuine, earthy kindness. They notice, and most often they come right back at you with the same brand of kindness.

I don't want to lose you in the first few days with any New Agey rap on the virtues of kindness, but you gotta admit, it's the easiest component of friendship and pretty much the best and most inexpensive gift you can give people.

ACTIVITY 4

You may be the type of gal who has no problem remembering every little date that matters to your friends. I'm not. I mean, I can remember my friend's birthday . . . month, but beyond that, I'm pretty hopeless. But that doesn't mean I don't care—I swear! And that is why this little exercise/craft is so practical as well as meaningful. Even if you do have a memory like an elephant's (they never forget!), this is still a fabulous way to kick-start your new outlook on friendship.

You're going to create a calendar with your friend or friends. There are plenty of ways to do this. You could go all tech and get a .Mac account and do it online. But you can't decorate it that way. And hello? Decorating is the frosting on the cupcake, the sprinkles on the fro-yo, the sweet spice in your teacup of life.

So go the way of either the blank day planner or the blank wall calendar. Purchase them at the office supply store, or download a template from the Internet and make your own on the cheap. Get with the girl(s) and your blank pages. If you're doing the downloaded thing, you can make just one calendar and photocopy it as many times as you have friends participating.

Go month by month. Talk about the month of January— parties coming up, days off and the like—and then move on to February. Mark down family birthdays, friends' birthdays, celebs' birthdays, wacky holidays to celebrate—I suggest Bad Poetry Day on August 18 and Seijin No Hi (Coming-of-Age Day in Japan!) on the second Monday in January.

Take photos of yourself and your friends and glue them all over the borders of the pages. Mark your birthday with your favorite picture of you. Doodle galore. Pick random days and mark them as "Celebrate Your Friends Day," and then when the time comes, do it! Celebrate your friends with a trip to the ice cream shop or a picnic or a roller-skating parade down your block. The point is to all be in possession of the *same exact calendar*.

SONG OF THE DAY:
STARS, "CALENDAR GIRL"
These Canadians deliver an uplifting and inspiring song that celebrates the glorious support of friendship throughout the months of the year. Even when things look bleak, the future represented in the calendar—and the friendship—delivers hope. Plus, Amy Millan's voice is fragility at its best.

DAY FIVE
THE GOOEY GUMDROP GLUE

Supportive vs. Unsupportive

Friendships are like bras,
Providing support and strength,
Uplifting the girls.

This is most often the stuff we crave when we crave our girlfriends: support.

And what happens when we don't get it? We feel lousy about ourselves, we feel lonely, we feel alone. Support is the glue of friendship, there's no denying it.

Support can come in the form of cheering you on or backing you up. But mostly, it's about listening with an attentive ear. Think about it—when you need support from your friends, do you really want them to fix your problem for you, *their* way? Or tell you it's no big deal and move on to the next subject? No and no.

Support is not saying "I told you so." It is not making light of your pals' feelings when they're bummed, and it's not blaming them or challenging them or even rescuing them. It's about listening and respecting and not passing judgment. It's not about you. It's about taking your friends seriously, even when you don't totally get it.

I don't think you should lean on your friends nonstop till they fall over. If you're doing that, you need full-on, full-time crutches, and that's different from friendly support. But when you're in need, your friends should be there. When the tables are turned and they are the ones in need, you should be there. Like so much in life, it's about balance.

Your friends should support you. You get that. But for everything? Anything? This is tricky territory. What if they are acting wildly inappropriate? Or full of rage? Or worse yet, they are hurting themselves or others? You try to get through to them by letting them know you're there. But they are making choices about how to behave, and maybe you need to make some hard choices as well.

What if a friend asks you to lie on her behalf? Is that support? Is telling her no, you won't lie, unsupportive? Ultimately, you have your own moral code, and your friends shouldn't ask you to break that or fake that. When a friend asks you to do something immoral or totally uncool in the name of "support," that friend is using you and your goodness. That friend isn't being a friend at all.

Ah, but there is another kind of support. The physical support that comes from standing by your friend, helping her attract the ones she wants and deflect those she does not. Curious? Read on.

• • •

ACTIVITY 5

There is nothing that makes me cringe more than when two friends fight over a guy. It's never, ever worth it. Our crushes come and go, piling up like trash in a landfill, but girlfriendship is long-term joy and support and kindness and every other chapter we're gonna work through in this book.

So that is why on this day of support, we're going to

throw that dangerous car ride into reverse. You're going to learn the supportive ways of the wingman—er, wingwoman. Like in *Top Gun*—remember when Tom Cruise was young and cute? And this leads me to an excellent point: boys don't fight over girls. They stand by their friend code.

What do you know—we can actually learn something from boys. Imagine that.

This activity illustrates how you can be a supportive friend during one of my favorite activities: flirting. But you can be a supportive wingwoman in other situations: when you're making new friends and when she's at your house hanging with your parents. When you get older, it's even fabulous for making excellent work contacts.

HOW TO BE A WINGWOMAN:

BOOST HER UP. Before you begin, remind her she's smart and adorable and funny. Remind her of all the reasons you adore her. Give her the confidence to give it a go.

MAKE HER LOOK COOL. Check her teeth for spinach. Talk up her mad skills. Laugh at her jokes. Lead her to an appropriate story to tell and then let her finish it.

KNOW YOUR MISSION. We always wanna be on our best game, but during this particular moment it's her time to shine, so keep that in mind and try hard not to take over.

RUN INTERFERENCE. If the object of your friend's affections has a guy friend stuck to his side, talk to the friend, distracting him from what's going on mere inches away. If another girl is stalking around, you can distract her as well—simply compliment her outfit and ask where she got her shoes.

GET HER OUT OF BAD SITUATIONS. If your friend is cornered by a jerk, feign sickness, pretend you are in desperate need of her presence, do whatever you've got to do to save her.

LIKE THE GAMBLER, YOU GOT TO KNOW WHEN TO WALK AWAY. Once things are going smoothly, that is your cue to excuse yourself and give them some space to talk.

Once you show your BFF the righteous ways of the wingwoman, my guess is she'll be so very inclined to return the favor.

SONG OF THE DAY:
GROOVE ARMADA, "MY FRIEND"
This dance tune's message is simple and repetitive, but that doesn't make it any less meaningful. The protagonist of the song calls on her friend whenever she's in need and her friend always, always comes round. That's support, baby.

Day Six
THE VERY DEFINITION OF FRIENDSHIP

Loyal vs. Disloyal

Hey, stand by your friend—
It is not girl vs. girl.
No competitions.

You know the expression "your loyal friend"? Well, is there really any other kind? Sort of, maybe. Because I've noticed more and more girls complaining about their friends' stabbing them in the back, telling their secrets, sneaking out with their boyfriends, yada yada blecch. So are they disloyal friends?

Or no friends at all?

I'm in the latter camp. I think loyalty and friendship go hand in hand, like Laverne and Shirley.

Simply put, if you can't be loyal, you can't be a good friend. And if you're loyal like the president's dog, then today's words will just make you feel even better about yourself and your super friendship wonder powers.

To be loyal means you are faithful, you can be trusted, you're reliable and what you say is true. Sounds like a definition of friendship to me. Your friends should be able to rely on you, and you on them. You should know that they are honest and caring and thoughtful, and they should know that of you.

If your "friends" have no problem talking trash about you when you're not around, they aren't being loyal, and they aren't being friends. If your "friends" are manipulating you to act a certain way or do things you don't want to do, then it's very clear to the rest of us that they aren't being friends. They are being something else. Frenemies? Users? Whatever. They are using their friendship powers for evil instead of good.

And you know why people continue to hang around with frenemies? It's easier than rocking the boat, shaking things up. And also, they get used to it. They get used to the bad behavior and see it as how a friend sometimes acts—as normal, even.

But it's not normal. And it's not okay.

Gossip, which we will discuss again and again in this book, is such an easy trap. And I'm betting that even the most saintly of us occasionally gossip about our friends. Usually, it's because talking about other people in a negative way can oddly make you feel better about yourself—I think that's ultimately why people gossip. That, and they like to hear the sound of their own voice. But you know it isn't worth it; that isn't the right way to feel better about yourself. A great way to feel good about yourself is to be a loyal friend and surround yourself with loyal friends. By resisting the urge to gossip, particularly about a friend, you will ultimately feel a whole lot better about yourself and feel more comfortable around those very friends. This is key: feeling good is not about bringing others down. You cannot judge yourself by other girls' successes . . . or failures.

The opposite of being loyal, really, is cheating. We talk of cheating when we do something disloyal to a boyfriend, but do we use that word when we do something disloyal to a girlfriend? Not usually. But that's what we're doing when we talk about our friends behind their backs, when we dis them to others, when we stand by them through the good times but walk straight away during the uncomfortable, awkward and sad times. We're cheating.

Defend your friends in their absence, stand by them when they're down, speak well of them behind their backs. Always act in their best interest, even if no one is looking. This is what it means to be loyal.

ACTIVITY 6

Write down the names of three friends in the spaces allotted on the next page. Under their names write down three ways they *need* you. Do they need your support in school? At a game? With a guy? Do they need a sympathetic ear to vent to about classes? Or family life? Do they need to know you care about their future? Their state of mind? The pressure they are feeling from others? Every one of us needs friends. So write down why your friends need YOU.

Next to that, I want you to think hard and dig deep and write down why you need them. Do they make you feel warm and fuzzy inside? Can you always count on them? Do they inspire you? Just make you laugh? Whatever it is, write it down.

Name: _____

She needs me to . . .   I need her to . . .

1. _____   1. _____

2. _____   2. _____

3. _____   3. _____

Name: _____

She needs me to . . .   I need her to . . .

1. _____   1. _____

2. _____   2. _____

3. _____   3. _____

Name: _____

She needs me to . . .   I need her to . . .

1. _____   1. _____

2. _____   2. _____

3. _____   3. _____

These are just some of the wonderful and varied aspects of friendship. Sometimes when we see the reciprocity of our girlfriend-ships, and the core needs, we are reminded of what is most important. Continue to ask yourself what it is about your friends that makes them so special, and continue to think about why you are such a great friend to them.

Now, if you can keep these things in the forefront of your mind and you can continue to be there for these girls, especially in these circumstances, you're being loyal. And it feels so much better to be that than to cheat.

SONG OF THE DAY:
THE THEME TO *THE GOLDEN GIRLS*
Thank you for being a friend . . . C'mon, you know I'm right—this is a righteous tune from a seriously awesome show about friends late in the game of life. In my *Golden Girls* future I'll be the statuesque Bea Arthur, my pal Karen is definitely racy Blanche, and Michelle is the wise yet dingy Betty White character.

day seven
GRACIAS, MERCI AND *DANKE SCHÖN*

Gratitude vs. the Ungrateful Snit

Without those two words
You are taking advantage.
Say it now: Thank you.

Gratitude—it's about saying thank you.

It's about doling out the love.

It's about acknowledging your pals and appreciating their spirit.

Man, I suck at this one.

I mean, I wait all year till it's someone's birthday to tell them how much they mean to me.

And it's not like I'm some ungrateful snit. I don't think I take advantage of my friends or their friendship. And I do give heaping helpings of thankfulness when I've been through a rough patch and they are there by my side.

But I also have some sort of mental block when it comes to letting them know I care on some random, everyday sort of day. Letting them know I am seriously thankful for their friendship during those plain ol' ordinary days is important.

Being truly ungrateful is taking advantage of your friends. When you take and take and take and never give anything back. I've had friends like that before. They expect that you'll be there for them no matter what, but they can't be bothered with your life's small things. It's draining and they're exhausting.

It's not that it needs to be so even Steven every day—like if you call needing me twice this week, you owe me two calls—because life isn't like that. Nobody is keeping score. It's an ebb and flow. One girl's good week is another girl's bad week. But you know the type of person who sucks up all the energy in the universe and then doesn't give any back, ever? That doesn't fly in the world of friendship.

How to Deal with . . .
The Fair-weather Friend

Do you have a friend who only calls you when she really needs you? Who only comes around when she wants something? It's so common that that type of friend even has a name: the fair-weather friend. She can be annoying, for sure. But as long as you realize that that's her role in your life—and provided you get some good friendship vibes back from her—this isn't the end of the world, nor does it have to be the end of the friendship. See, the fair-weather friend doesn't make a good BFF—to earn that distinction you need loyalty and supportiveness and the other qualities I've been rattling off in this book. But not all friends are meant to be BFFs, or even close buds. Some are meant to drift in and out of your life. They complement your relationships, they don't replace them. Think of those types of friendships as the condiments at your girlfriend-ship dinner table. Don't expect that that ketchup is going to fill you up or satisfy your hunger. But ain't it nice to dip your fries in there from time to time? Even though your fair-weather friend is coming at you when she needs something, you may be getting something out of it too. Maybe the sensation of being needed, maybe the satisfaction of being supportive, maybe the spark of something new . . . or maybe not.

ACTIVITY 7

To make sure we are doling out the love in a continuous and wholly random way, I bring you Thanksgiving in July (or February or April or whenever)! You don't get a bunch of days off for this one—this is a Friendship Thanksgiving.

So, gather a friend or three over for a Thanksgiving dinner (or lunch). Don't cook? Don't freak—simply serve **Turkey-and-Cranberry-and-Stuffing Sandwiches!**

INGREDIENTS
- A small box of instant stuffing mix (like Stove Top)
- Four hearty rolls
- A can of cranberry sauce (preferably the chunky kind and not that weird Jell-O-like substance)
- One pound of deli turkey

DIRECTIONS
Prepare the stuffing according to package directions. It can usually even be made in the microwave. Split the rolls in half; spread a tablespoon or more of the cranberry sauce on the bread like jam. Pile a quarter of the turkey onto each roll. Top with a quarter-cup or more of hot, freshly made stuffing. Close up sandwich and serve!

And please don't forget the pie. It's not Thanksgiving without pie. Pick one up in the freezer section at your grocery store or hit a bakery—and remember to get some whipped cream.

BONUS EXERCISE

As an extra bonus, you can present your guests with their own **THANKSGIVING WREATHS OF LOVE.** Here's how:

....

It's time to take a trip back to second grade. Do you remember ever making a thankful wreath in November? You'll need a *paper plate, construction or scrapbook paper* in fall colors (orange, yellow, red, brown), *glue, scissors* and a *pen.*

Cut the center out of the plate so that you have a circle or "wreath" to build on. Now cut leaf shapes from your colored paper. Find a nice one for the top center. On that leaf write "I am thankful for your . . . " Glue it down. And then on the remaining leaves write the things you are indeed thankful for—all the wonderful reasons your pal is such a good friend. Write things like "Laughter" and "Intelligence" and "Caring." Glue the leaves to the wreath, slightly overlapping them but making sure they are still readable. Present the wreaths to your pals and watch them tear up with preschool memories, laughter and gratitude.

SONG OF THE DAY:

NATALIE MERCHANT, "KIND & GENEROUS"

Quite possibly the sweetest thank-you ever recorded in song. Play this one on a loop during your Thanksgiving feast. Sing and sway along. Everyone, now . . . "La la la la la la la la."

DaY EIGHT
DO-GOODERS AND
DON'T-GOODERS

Integrity vs. Disgrace

Temptation to sway,
To do stupid, stupid things . . .
Avoid the kegger.

Integrity is something we don't talk about too much. It may seem odd in this first chapter, near kindness and openness and gratitude. But I tell you what: I can look around at all my friends—they are different shapes and sizes, come from different walks of life, have different backgrounds and belief systems—but all my good friends have this one thing in common. No, not great hair (although, oddly, that is a common thread as well). I'm talking about integrity, of course.

"There can be no friendship without confidence, and no confidence without integrity."

Samuel Johnson said that. He was an eighteenth-century British poet.

Soundness of moral character—that's how "integrity" is defined. It can't be seen, and it's often hard to describe.

I guess in its most simple form it means you're honest. But it's even more than that. To me it means something bigger—you care about the world and you respect yourself and you conduct your life in a way that illustrates that very care and respect. It means making good choices, or at least trying to. We don't always make the perfect choice, but when we strive to, that's integrity.

Having friends with integrity makes life a lot easier, because you trust them. When you have friends who don't respect themselves or others, it can get embarrassing. Or worse, disgraceful. They can get in heaps of trouble when they aren't being truthful to you, others or themselves. They can ultimately get you in trouble. And when people are making bad choices all around you, it can be that much harder to make good choices yourself. All that disgraceful crud can rub off on you like poison ivy hidden in clover. So, like the ivy, it should be avoided. Disgracefulness can hold you back and trip you up.

But integrity? Well, that can inspire wonderful things large and small.

ACTIVITY 8

Grab a friend. Ask her what is important to her in the world. Ask yourself the same question. Talk about what you two can do together to make a difference in the world. And then make a plan.

Here are a few starting places. Dream big, girls.

TAKE A VOLUNTEER JOB AT THE LOCAL HUMANE SOCIETY OR LIKE-MINDED INSTITUTION. You get to play with the animals, be with your friend and give back to humanity all in one afternoon. Way to use your time wisely.

RUN A 5K FOR A CHARITY. There are 5Ks in most major cities every month. If you're not ready to run that far just yet (it's a little over three miles), start getting in shape now for next month or the month after, and do so with a friend. Each run usually supports a different cause, such as leukemia research or literacy.

PREP FOR A TWO-DAY WALK FOR BREAST CANCER. This is the monster of all walkathons—two days, thirty-nine miles, but totally life-changing. All proceeds go to breast cancer research. So grab your friends (and probably a mom) and make a plan. The walks occur throughout the year in major cities across America. It may be months away, but you have to train for something of this magnitude.

KNIT SWEATERS. Grab a girlfriend, attend a knitting workshop, learn the basics and then set out to knit a sweater or two or a bunch of hats over the next six months. Donate them to one of the many organizations that collect winter wear for needy children around the world. Or make a quilt with your friends and donate the cozy warmth of a new blanket.

COLLECT CANNED FOOD FOR A LOCAL SHELTER. Or collect lightly used teddy bears for an orphanage. Or business suits for women reentering the workforce. Find your cause, define a need, and go out there and get to it. I guarantee you'll have fun, since you'll be working with your best bud, and you'll feel phenomenal having made a difference in someone else's life.

Other Ideas: _____

_____

_____

_____

SONG OF THE DAY:
ME FIRST AND THE GIMME GIMMES,
"YOU'VE GOT A FRIEND"
This classic Carole King song is interpreted by the punk-rock cover kings. In this incarnation it is a fast and furious ode to finding the bright light of friendship in the darkest times. Turn it up to 11.

HOW TO MAKE
FRIENDSHIPS EVEN
BETTER:
THE GO-BEYOND

We've now covered the basics of friendship, as far as I'm concerned. But is it enough? Can you do more?

Learn more?

Be more?

You know my answer is an astounding and painfully loud YES!

What follows are the concepts and ideals that dig deeper into the heart of what friendship is. Remember, not every friend is meant to be lifelong. Don't get me wrong; I believe they should all have the basic qualities of honesty and loyalty. But what of those close friends, the ones we want as our big BFFs? For those, well, these are concepts and qualities that will take you there.

Day Nine
FUTURE TALK-SHOW HOSTS, UNITE!

Communication Star vs. the Nontalker

Let's talk about love,
Politics, feelings and life,
And, of course, shoes too.

There are a zillion types of friends. But we can also divide them all into two categories: those you share things with and those you don't.

Why is it that you don't really get to the heart of life with some friends? Talking about the world, important personal matters, your own issues and problems and dreams, all forge a closer connection to others. And when we don't open up about any of these things, we simply stay on the surface.

I know guys who can spend an entire day together and not talk about anything important. They just grunt and comment on things they see in front of their faces at that moment in time. We all know guys like this.

We don't expect the same behavior from our girl-friends, and yet look around—we do it too. Our conversation is about her dress or his shoes or the food in front of us. We can go whole entire days without talking about what's going on in our minds and hearts.

If you are looking to go beyond basic camaraderie, the very first thing you need to do is talk about real-life stuff. You can start with your own stuff, but you can't rely on just you talking. You need to ask questions. You need to delve deeper—let your friends know that their lives are interesting to you. When you open up to someone you trust, and you show them that trust, they in turn will probably open up to you.

Maybe the mall isn't the place to do this; maybe that is where we talk shoes and clothes and food. Or maybe not. Maybe it's the perfect place to talk about real-life issues because you're comfortable and at ease and not under any pressure to have BIG talks, the way you might if you were to do this under some designated "moment of truth."

And that, I guess, is my point: start small. It doesn't have to come in one big long gush. It doesn't have to be some made-for-TV moment. Just really get to know your friends through dialogue, over time. And equally important, let them get to know you.

When you ask questions, you challenge assumptions. You're saying "I'm not going to just assume this is so, I'm going to ask you how you really feel." That is respect, baby. It can be very exciting.

A friend who you can celeb-gossip with (not the evil kind of gossip, mind you), and shop with, and that's it, can be fun. But chances are, you will grow up and away from them. You and a friend who you can delve deeper with and who knows you backward and forward may also grow apart in your hobbies and tastes, but the connections will remain. And so will the meaningful friendship.

How to Deal with . . .
The Girl Who Can't Keep a Secret

Remember, not every friend is going to be the one you tell your secrets to. And that is okay. You should have different types of friends—the ones who simply make you giggle till it hurts, the ones who get your guy problems, the ones who inspire you to try harder at school or work, the ones who would enjoy an afternoon at the museum and the ones who are simply fun to shop with. Just make sure to keep the private things from the girl who has a history of telling, and you won't be setting yourself up for disappointment.

ACTIVITY 9

Okay, you're saying "I know that I'm supposed to talk about meaningful stuff, but like what? And how?" Here are some prompts, some questions to ask the other person and to ask yourself. I'm not opposed to inviting a friend or two over for a slumber party and breaking out the popcorn and writing the questions on little slips of paper like some crazy parlor game. If you and your friends are feeling that, by all means . . . but don't think that it's all got to happen in one big night.

And don't pummel your friends with the questions one after the other. It will sound like an interview—or worse, an interrogation. And for crying out loud, listen when they answer you.

This is just the tip of the iceberg, a few questions to get you thinking about the kinds of things you might want to ask. Once you get going, I suspect you'll be curious about aspects of one another that will lead to new questions.

- Do you have a secret dream? Something you want to achieve or do? In the next five years? Ten years? Your lifetime? Where did this dream come from? What spurred it?

- What do you never want to do? Have you ever had to do anything you wish you could have gotten out of?

- What's the best advice you ever got?

- Is there something you cannot live without?

- If you could have dinner with anyone in the world, living or dead, who would it be?

- Where would you go if you went into hiding?

- What is the craziest thing you ever did?

- What was your best family vacation? And of course, why?

- If you could help anyone in the world, who would it be?

- Were you named after anyone?

- If you could go anywhere in the world, where would you go?

- Did you ever have an imaginary friend?

If it's really difficult for you to do this sort of thing, you could get one of those *All About You* books or one of the *If . . .* (*Questions for the Game of Life*) books and read from it together. These books are filled with interesting questions and scenarios, and your and your friends' answers will tell a lot about your deeper selves.

Alternatively, you could write up one of those e-mails with questions like the aforementioned, as well as things like "What's your favorite cereal?" and "If you were a crayon color, what would you be?" and pass them around. But don't use e-mail to talk. Make one of the more interesting answers a starting place for a conversation the next time you're together.

And here is the most important part of this exercise: don't share the information you've learned about your friend with others. It's not about being secretive and alienating other friends because you know *more*. We don't ever want to make any of our friends feel bad. It's about respecting your friend and not passing on information that she shared with you that she simply may not want others to know.

SONG OF THE DAY:
WEEZER, "MY BEST FRIEND"

There is nothing ironic about this song from these L.A. nerdy rock boys; it's a straightforward tune about friendship, love and gratitude. This should be at the top of everyone's mix CD for their best pal.

DAY TEN
A GLASS HALF-FULL

Optimism vs. Pessimism

Which sounds like more fun?
Complaining and bitching, or
Loving and laughing?

Are you a glass-half-full girl? Or half-empty? What about your close friends?

Half-full folks are peppy, look at life like an adventure, go for it with gusto.

Half-empty girls are negative, appear to be struggling all the time and bring others down with them.

Which is why it matters whether you and your friends are in fact half-full or half-empty, optimists or pessimists. Like so many other things in this book, your outlook is contagious. The pessimist drags everyone around them into the dark and nether regions of, at best, boredom and, at worst, depression.

And the optimist inspires and ignites the fire within others. Unless of course they're optimistic to the point of the over-the-top, faux-Miss-Teen-America-Vaseline-smile speech, and then they're simply annoying. But never mind, it still may be better than having a Donnie Darko as your BFF.

If you're a pessimist, now is the optimum time to explore why. Are you just more comfortable plopped down in the middle of the mud? Do you feel smarter by being dark and skeptical? (I've been guilty of that wack misconception.) Or are you really unhappy? No matter where you're coming from, I think I know where you should be going—you need to find your passion and your purpose. (Oprah alert! Oprah alert!) But seriously, you need to force yourself to do something unexpected and joyful. Challenge yourself to be positive and try something new, something that mildly interests you, and come out the other side actively thinking about what just occurred. Don't know how to do that? Read on to Activity 10.

If your pal is the pessimist, well, they have to do their own changing. But certainly it would show great friendship and care if you created an opportunity or two for her to challenge those feelings that are telling her life is only handing out lemons and sour lemonade. Get your pal to see that there is goodness around her (that's you!) and to recognize and acknowledge when good things happen. Remind her to put herself in some new situations that will have really lovely outcomes. If she is willing to take the leap into uncharted territory, she could possibly, maybe come out happier on the other side.

See, you can't touch it, yet optimism has the ability to

lift you up even when you got nothin'. Because you can always, always find hope and expectation inside yourself, even when you can't, at that moment in time, find a good friend.

ACTIVITY 10

The five senses—seeing, hearing, smelling, tasting and touching—can bring us pleasure . . . and pain. They are the impetus, the triggers to our feelings and memories. Today we are looking for unexpected joy; we are trying to uncover the little things that bring us that unique kind of happiness that makes us feel alive and, yes, optimistic. This is where you start.

On the next page, write down things you enjoy seeing, hearing, smelling, tasting and touching. As you make your list, really take your time and think about each individual sense for a moment. Try to smell the thoughts that waft through your head as you think about SMELL and imagine the sensation in your mouth as you think of the things you love to TASTE.

SIGHT

1. _____
2. _____
3. _____
4. _____
5. _____
6. _____
7. _____
8. _____
9. _____

SOUND

1. _____
2. _____
3. _____
4. _____
5. _____
6. _____
7. _____
8. _____
9. _____

SMELL

1. _____
2. _____
3. _____
4. _____
5. _____
6. _____
7. _____
8. _____
9. _____

TASTE

1. _____
2. _____
3. _____
4. _____
5. _____
6. _____
7. _____
8. _____
9. _____

TOUCH

1. _____
2. _____
3. _____
4. _____
5. _____
6. _____
7. _____
8. _____
9. _____

Now you can connect two or three things from different columns into one activity. For instance, under SOUND I have "Wilco playing ridiculously loud on my headphones" and under SMELL I wrote "freshly cut grass." And under TOUCH I have written "the pavement under my feet." I can combine those three things into a solitary walk through the neighborhood with my iPod cranked to 11. And that little exercise is complete and utter joy . . . to me. Yours will be different.

Maybe you'll write "punk rock" under SOUND and "metallic strings" under TOUCH and "me, tossing my hair" under SIGHT, and voila! You will be led to guitar lessons, preferably electric. Or perhaps you will write down "cake batter" under SMELL *and* TASTE, and you may think the idea of touching a cake doesn't sound half bad either. Your joy may be in the act of creating two layers. Let the list and your senses lead you to newfound joys.

After you try this new thing, come back to this page and ask yourself: "Did I enjoy myself? Did life actually feel more comfortable and cozy there for a moment? Do I feel pride? Love? Respect?" Well, harness that nuggy-nug of goodness, whatever it is, and tell yourself "This is what optimism and joy feel like."

SONG OF THE DAY:
SONIC YOUTH, "MY FRIEND GOO"
Kim Gordon sings this silly nineties art-punk ode to her friend "Goo." I bet Kim's an awesome friend. This is one to cover in that new band you're gonna start any day now, natch.

DAY ELEVEN
GOAL GIRL

Achiever vs. Partier

Exhibit A: Lindsay.
She has goals, but she has strayed—
Far too many boys.

Okay, they are not mutually exclusive. You can be a partier and still have goals. But if the partying is not done in moderation, the goals slowly fall by the wayside. Having goals gives you focus. Focus on the bigger picture and all that life has to offer you, not just on where the next party is.

Even if your buds aren't classic goal-oriented, straight-A girls, they should still have that vision to be able to see beyond the weekend. Because otherwise, they can get too wrapped up in the really petty stuff of life. I once had a friend who really did live for the next big bang because of the boys. She was looking for a guy to change her life—she thought if she found the right one, her life would be different and, ergo, wonderful. She was looking to this unknown idealized person to awaken her life and move it along.

Goal girls use their brains, their intuition, their agility and their passion to move life forward. They don't just wait for life to happen or for someone to come and change their world for them. They do it themselves. Of course, as the Beatles said, a little help from your friends is okay too.

In fact, when we share our goals with our friends, when we talk about them out loud, as opposed to keeping them balled up inside us, we are more likely to follow through because we are more accountable, having told someone else about them. It's almost like sharing them makes them more real.

Remember that your goals, like your outlook on life, should be flexible. They are not written in **stone** or in blood. They may change over time (they probably will), and that is A-OK too. Because it's not just about the result; it's also about the process. And along the way you will discover new things about yourself, life, your dreams and more, and those things will inform and inspire new goals. It isn't just about getting to the finish line and yelling "GOOOOAAAAALLLLLLLL!" like they do in soccer. It's about the whole journey.

ACTIVITY 11

I'm a visual person. I think in pictures. The problem with being a visual person is that if, say, a box of crackers is in the cupboard, I simply forget it's there. I need to *see* it out on the counter so as to herald the crackers' delicious presence.

Which is why I bring you the Vision Map. In the advertising world, this is called a "mood board." In an office setting it's a tool to work up the look and feel of a brand, from which the designers then brainstorm. Essentially, you take a bunch of magazine pictures and words that represent the idea and you glue them on the classic elementary school material: poster board. My pal Keva used to do these for a big-time ad agency. (Yep, she made collages for her job!)

And now you're going to do it—but not for a product. Rather, you are doing this for your own dreams and vision and goals.

You'll need the aforementioned *poster board,* some basic *Elmer's-type glue* and a stack of *old magazines.*

Look through the magazines for pictures and words

that inspire you. And if you have specific goals, hunt down images and words that represent them—a college catalog, for instance, will have photos of the campus or the library. If you long to work for a particular newspaper or company, hunt down words and images that signify those places.

And don't just look at your career goals—also think about the feelings you are working toward, like self-sufficiency, peace, joy, respect, responsibility. Glue these pictures to your own poster board or foam-core board.

Around the perimeter, paste pictures of your support group—your friends and family and mentors who can and will give you that little boost when you need it (and we all need it sometimes).

And when you're done, put it in plain sight in your room—next to your bed or propped up on your desk. That way you can see it every day and your dreams won't go stale—like the sorry box of crackers in my cupboard.

And Another Thing . . .

This is a great project to do alone or with a friend. When you make a Vision Map with a friend, you're opening up yourself and your dreams to that girl-friend, and she is doing likewise. It can be a beautiful bonding experience and a whole lot of fun. But if you aren't ready to share this side of you and you want to use this opportunity to cultivate your goals and your insides, then by all means sail this one solo.

SONG OF THE DAY:
WILCO, "WHAT LIGHT"

My all-time favorite band sings a rare (for them) superpositive song. It's an inspiring one that urges you to look inside yourself for the strength to do what pleases you and makes you happy. Play this one when you're feeling a bit low and need a lift.

DAY TWELVE
FAUX FRIENDS

Being the Real You vs. Being a Faker

Insecurity blows,
Makes you be something you're not—
Like a wannabe.

You can ask my little brother—he will happily share stories of my wayward youth. He'll tell you I tried everything in my power to *not* be me so that I would fit in. It's a common story, and many a teen movie has been filmed with this as the premise. In an effort to be liked and "popular," I traded my beliefs for someone else's. It didn't last all that long, though.

Because it's way hard to keep that crap up.

I'm not even talking about straight-up lying so much as just misrepresenting. Faking. I made nice to people who were mean; I wore the clothes that were considered "cool" even if they weren't exactly my style and I didn't feel comfortable in them; I didn't tell anyone about my love of sixties soul music because at the time back in my hometown of Hollywood, Florida, everyone was listening to Southern-fried radio rock.

But think about it: those girls I was friends with at that time didn't even know the real me. So they weren't friends with the real me. They were friends with some facsimile of me that still had my tweaked-out frizzy hair but that wore lots of plaid, listened to plastic pop and talked about boys incessantly.

Do you want to be friends with someone's fake self? Do you want to be that kind of friend to someone else? Of course not. You're smarter than I ever was.

It's okay to be different from your friends. You don't have to all be named Heather or dress the same or look the same or even like the same things. But it's more acceptable now than when I was younger—I mean, look at *The Sisterhood of the Traveling Pants*. Four girls, great friends, all way different. I know it's a work of fiction, but it isn't that far from reality. It's not so unusual anymore. It's your quirks that make you *you* and ultimately make you a more interesting friend. If the other girls don't get that, they aren't looking for real friends. They are looking for clones. And you know how I feel about that.

Like some former teen actor who can't get an acting job as an "adult" even though he's now twenty-
five, we too can get typecast, or stereotyped as
being one thing—the nerd, the dumb blonde, the
goth, the kid. But of course, even though our
essence may not change, over time we evolve.
We are each certainly more than just one-word
stereotypes. And sometimes all you want to do is
reinvent yourself so that you can get far away from
the role your friends or family have ascribed to
you. Is reinventing yourself being fake? Not if that
person you want to become is the real you. When
I went to college and got miles from my family, I
was really able to be me—I wasn't the preppy big
sister to my brother; I wasn't the sad, depressed
teen my mom decided I was; and I wasn't the poor
girl from the bad neighborhood at my school. Once
I was away, I was me: sixties-soul-music-loving, flip-
flop-wearing, politically active, big-haired me!

ACTIVITY 12

Nothing breaks down false walls and removes lacquered
faux sheens like laughter, particularly when the laughter
is aimed squarely at ourselves. If you want to try to cut
through the crud, grab your girlfriend and get goofy in
the name of "good fun." Here are five stomach-busting,
giggleworthy go-go things to do together:

1. TAKE AN ART CLASS. Make it a nude art class. No, you're not painting in the nude, the model is nude. It is most definitely awkward in the beginning, but sit tight and try your hand at painting. You will learn about the human body, how it moves and how it is portrayed in paint. Give it a real try, and afterward, you and your friend can marvel at your attempts and giggle at the absurdity of a naked person's getting paid to sit still for an hour while you girls stared.

2. TRY ON BRIDESMAID DRESSES. Go ahead and tell the salesgirl you two are going to be bridesmaids and need two matching dresses . . . in mint green! Yes, it is lying, but it doesn't hurt anyone, provided you are careful with the dresses and don't damage them or get them dirty. Crack up over the craziness of wearing matching mint green outfits. Bring a camera and ask the salesgal to take your picture together so that you can run the dresses by the "bride" for approval.

3. TRY MODERN DANCE. Have you ever watched a modern dance class? They are a blur of wacky moves, frenetic music and high leg kicks. Throw all reservations and ego out the door before you set foot into this class. Resolve to give it a real try and not make fun of the people around you; just enjoy the kookiness of it all. And if by chance one or both of you is a modern dance savant, skip this one and do something else. This is only for girls who *can't* dance.

4. RUN OFF AND JOIN THE CIRCUS. Or rather, the circus school. There are a ton of them out there now, thanks to the vast popularity of Cirque du Soleil. They offer instruction on tightrope walking, trapeze artistry and even clowning. Wear ridiculous circuslike attire for extra ha-has.

5. OFFER TO BE HAIR MODELS. Most beauty schools, from the basic ones to the fancy Sassoon ones, have hair shows, and they need models. Basically you agree to let them do anything to your hair except cut it. Many hair shows go big and go wacky—birdcages entwined in hair, gigantic bee-hives, crazy faux-hawks, that sort of thing. Get your do's done and then strut your stuff on the catwalk together. And best of all, it's free!

SONG OF THE DAY:
THE REMBRANDTS, "I'LL BE THERE FOR YOU"
Otherwise known as the *Friends* theme song, this is a mega-cheesy tune. But everyone knows it's goofy as all get-out, and if you can find a fountain, you and your pal(s) can awkwardly dance around in it like Jennifer Aniston and company did.

Day Thirteen
I, ME, MINE!

Empathy vs. Self-Absorption

Walk in someone's shoes
So you can see what she sees.
Wow, it hurts my eyes.

In a study done in 2006 in London, teenagers and adults were given specific scenarios and then asked for their reactions. As they responded, researchers watched their brain activity. The teens' and adults' brain activity were different, as were their responses. The conclusion was that teens and young adults simply don't use the area of the brain that is associated with empathy. It wasn't found that they *can't,* or that that particular area of the brain isn't fully formed; it was that, by and large, they just don't use that part of the brain.

Empathy is when you try to see someone else's life

from their perspective. It's hard to really digest this, but you've got to know, not everyone sees the world from the same place as you do. They have their own histories to contend with. People don't live on half-hour television shows where when the TV goes off, they go off too. No, when they are out of your sight, your friends continue with life and everything that goes along with that—their own families' influence, their upbringing, the voices in their head. And I guarantee, even if you dress the same and look the same and seem the same as your friends, what's going on in your heads ain't the same. Our minds are like snowflakes, each one delicately different.

What's the danger in not realizing this? In friendships it can lead to major misunderstandings, which can lead to the inability to support your pals in the way they most need it. If we don't develop our empathy, we become narrow-minded, and worse, so self-involved we can't relate to others, deal with others, be friends with others. Empathy is pretty much the key to a meaningful friendship, but it's also key to just being a functioning human being in the world today.

Another study—this one done even more recently than the last—said that text-messaging, e-mailing and instant-messaging, because they're written forms of communication, tend to provoke a deeper understanding than simply talking, and therefore inspire more empathy. So perhaps teen empathy will soon be on the rise. . . .

ACTIVITY 13

Hi, I'm your host, Clea Hantman. Welcome to another episode of Trading Spaces, *where two friends switch rooms and redecorate on a limited budget. Let's go meet our friends. C'mon . . .*

We're gonna trade spaces with a friend. Yeah, sort of like that silly TV show that's still on cable. But unlike that show, where they do things for shock value and faux exciting TV viewing, we're gonna actually try to give our friend a room that is appropriate for her and not just wacky, or simply pretty *to you*. Did you get that part? It's not about your tastes or needs, it's about your friend's.

If you still live at home, make sure you check with all the parental units and get their blessing (and maybe even their help!). Then get with your friend and start asking each other questions about your rooms. Because afterward, you're going to literally change rooms for the night and rearrange and introduce new items that will benefit your pal's lifestyle. What kinds of questions will get you the right kinds of answers? How 'bout these?

Where do you study or read? _____

_____

_____

What kind of light do you need/want for that? _____

_____

_____

_____

Do you like to sleep against the wall? Facing a certain way?

_____

_____

What do you do in this room besides sleep? Do you exercise? Do yoga? Hang out? _____

_____

_____

Are you still loving these colors? Or do you have a new fave?

_____

_____

Are you a visual person like Clea and need your stuff out and about? Or do you prefer it put away and hidden? _____

_____

If there were one thing you could change about your room, what would it be? What is your favorite thing about your room? _____

_____

And is there anything you would never want to change?

_____

Enlist some extra help in the form of roommates, siblings or other friends for each team. Set a budget. This can be zero and just involve moving things around and making a few small odds and ends. Or you can put a small budget on the project and each pony up $25 for supplies.

THINGS YOU CAN DO

- Think about which objects are meaningful to your friend, and put those front and center.

- If you have a small budget, you can paint a dresser or desk. (Unlike on *Trading Spaces*, you're gonna ask first.)

- Get a couple of books on storage and small-space decorating from the library. Clean. Organize. These things always make big impressions and are welcomed by most everyone.

- Curtains are fine, especially if your pal needs her privacy, but if not, you can get window decals or even vinyl letters and spell out an inspirational message.

- Pick up some stretched canvas at an art store and paint a picture just for her. Or blow up photos way big on the Xerox machine at your local copy store. Or get a bulletin board and cover it with cute fabric (maybe it matches some pillows you sew too).

- If she's in need of storage, go under the bed. Pick up a few boxes that you can stash stuff in, label them and slide them under the mattress frame. It's a great place for seasonal clothes like sweaters or for craft supplies.

- Don't discount the power of the basket. True, a bunch of straw ones on a shelf is a bit too country cabin for anyone under the age of seventy-five, but baskets are cheap, and with a coat of spray paint in a fun color they can be transformed into something with much more pop.

- Cover shoe boxes with cute wrapping paper to make in- and out-boxes for her desk, or places to keep her knick-knacks, paddywhacks and hair gigglies. Or paint coffee cans to create pretty vessels to hold stuff. Clean old spaghetti jars to hold pencils and pens on the desk. Look in the recycling bin—are there other things that can be rescued and repurposed for décor or storage? Get creative, get dirty, get busy.

Oh yeah, and no snooping.

SONG OF THE DAY:
THE REPLACEMENTS, "I'LL BE YOU"
This song really speaks to a frustration with being in a rut and to the feeling we all get sometimes that it would just be easier to switch places with someone. You know, the whole "the grass is greener" scenario. Probably not so, but it's still a damn fine song.

Day Fourteen
GRANDMA KNOWS BEST

Patience vs. Impatience

It's a waiting game,
But we want stuff quick and fast—
From burgers to friends.

Patience is a virtue, or so it is written on many a grandma's needlepoint sampler. Patience is also a necessary part of a good life. Because not everything comes as quickly as the chicken nuggets at the drive-through or the instant digi-pictures on our camera. And certainly friendship takes time to grow and deepen.

Don't get me wrong, there are people you meet and it's like—*bam!*—friendship at first sight. You just click with them instantly and know you will be buds. But even those friends take time to get to really know. And just be-cause there is that instant connection doesn't mean the friendship will be better than one that takes some warming-up time. (FYI, same goes for the "*love* at first sight" scenario—and those insta-connections usually burn out faster than birthday candles at a two-year-old's party.)

You have to remember that real relationships need experiences to deepen them, not just feelings. And experiences happen over time. Experiences like the ones you will set out to have tomorrow. The impatient girl who wants to be best friends right now and can't wait and needs to be with you 24-7 runs the risk of being clingy, needy and ultimately annoying. Be yourself, but don't forget to breathe. You don't have to be with someone all the time to be her friend. Take the time to be alone occasionally and enjoy the quiet and the comfort of you. Know that it's perfectly normal and right-on for friendships to take time.

81

Do you know one of those clingy types? The girl who has to have you to herself? She is henceforth known as the Possessive Friend. She won't share you; she speaks poorly of your other friends; she tries to make you see that she's the only one for you. But friendship doesn't work that way, and by now, on this, Day Fourteen, you already know that. Friendship, even when it's close-knit and so okely-dokely special, isn't about excluding others, and it's not about keeping one another penned up in a friendship cage. To be good friends, we need to experience the world and other people. This behavior usually stems from jealousy and a fear that if we don't keep tabs on our friends at all times, they will find someone better. And if you are in possession of a possessive friend, let her know that you care and you're close but that you both need to trust in the friendship as you explore the world.

ACTIVITY 14

Take some time out for yourself. I know, this is a book about friendships, and you're probably thinking, "I need to be with friends! Trying to win them over! Or hanging with them always!" But it doesn't really work like that. Because time alone is superimportant to make you the best *you* possible. And when you're the best you possible, it will be that much easier to win—and keep—friends.

So today's activity involves doing something for yourself, by yourself. We'll call it Celebrating You so that it has a nice partylike ring to it. Essentially I want you to write down some of the things you've done for others—activities in this book and things you've just done on your own. Did you smile at some strangers? Did you really take the time to listen to a friend? Jot it down. Did you do something nice for yourself recently? Jot that down too, because even though it is corny, you are always going to be your own best friend. They don't have to be big things; in fact, this should be about celebrating the small moments of life—they are the ones that make the world go round and the days pass into nights. I want you to take inventory of your own great friendship qualities. And don't skimp; really dig deep for all the interactions over the last two weeks that have meant something to you.

ACCOMPLISHMENTS

_____

_____

_____

_____

_____

NICE THINGS YOU DID FOR YOURSELF

_____

_____

_____

_____

_____

In that blank space next to the things you've written down I want you to draw a picture. I don't care if you don't think you can draw; you're not getting graded on this. I want you to draw a picture that expresses how you're feeling today and how you are feeling about the things you just wrote down. If you want to go all mixed media on me, you can—cut out pictures from a magazine and do it collage-style, even on a separate piece of paper. But really think about the different emotions you've experienced over the last couple of weeks. When you're done you can move on to the next page and forget about it for a while. And when you remember and you return to it, read it again and revel in all that is you and your fine self.

SONG OF THE DAY:
CYNDI LAUPER, "TIME AFTER TIME"
A gorgeous song of a friendship morphing and changing over time. After you play this one, throw on Lauper's "Girls Just Want to Have Fun" and dance, dance, dance like mad alone in your room.

DAY FIFTEEN
RUT-BUSTING REBELS

Effortlessly Amused vs. Boring Buds

Blah Blah Blah Blah Blah
Blah Blah Blah Blah Blah Blah Blah
Blah Blah Blah Bo-ring!

Boredom can eat away at a friendship like termites at a house. You don't even know those little buggers are there until your house starts to fall apart around you. Ruts just seem to sneak up on you too, and then before you know it, everyone's cranky and uninspired and blaming each other for the lack of fun. But fun often must be sought out.

It doesn't have to be in the form of big and grand parties. The best kind of fun starts small and becomes big by its sheer ability to surprise you, take down your guard and make you giggle.

Not everyone has the ability to think up wacky things to

do when the must-dos are all done. Businesspeople call this thinking *inside* the box—ideas that are all traditional and linear and go from point A to point B—or straight-line thinking. When you get two people together who think like that it can be hard to come up with exciting new stuff and way easy to fall into the boredom blues, the "we are doing the same stuff over and over" trap.

But even if you're the queen of "I dunno what to do," you can bust the rut. You just have to steer clear of the places and things you usually do, and you may need some outside prompting. But the point is, *get prompted*—allow yourself to look and think outside the box. Stay away from the mall. Don't go to your local hangouts. Try something really and truly new to you.

On That Note . . .

You can either be a "bring the fun" kind of girl or the girl who expects to be entertained. Who would you rather hang out with? Face it, you don't need others to come up with ideas when you have the ability to have fun wherever you go! Don't sit back and wait for others to make you happy . . . make the happy wherever, whenever.

ACTIVITY 15

This is easy, and yet so not. Your activity of the day is to take the things you normally do and spice them up, mix them round and round till they are different, unexpected and fun again. The result may not be something you want to keep doing; it may not be perfect. It may be just the first step. But you'll have succeeded if you've tried. Because usually, one new little thing will lead you to another until you've found that special something that shakes you from your rut and busts it wide open.

So, what do you normally do? Do you . . .

Go to a coffee shop? Then go to a different one. Invite along new friends. Order different drinks. Bring a deck of cards or a board game.

Go to the movies? Hit the indie theater in town, the one that shows only small films with big messages. Afterward, go somewhere with your pals and discuss the movie and what it meant and if you liked it. Or rent a bunch of oldies-but-goodies and make it an occasion—get cozy in pj's and sleeping bags or go glam and dress up and serve fancy snacks.

Go bowling? Fine—if you like bowling, keep bowling. But there is nothing that says you can't all dress exactly the same or completely ridiculously in crazy outfits. There is nothing that says you have to play by the rules. Make up your own!

Go to concerts? I love music, all kinds of music. Get out and see classical concerts in the park, fiddlers in the town square, punk-rock kids at the local rec center, folkies at the coffee shops and hair-metal bands from the eighties at the big stadium. Make it your mission to see five different types of bands in a month. Heck, you could even make it a scavenger hunt for instruments. Can you see an accordion band within the next thirty days? It's a challenge!

Go to (boring) parties? Throw your own, big or small. What's the occasion? It's Wednesday. Or the sun is shining. Or look up wacky holidays online and find one that's coming up and celebrate it in style. Whatever it is, make it random, come up with silly games and a fun food to go along with said theme and be prepared for anything.

Write down some other things you and your friends do often, and then below that, think about ways you can mix it up!

Go to _____

_____

_____

_____

Go to _____

_____

_____

_____

Whatever it is you normally do, twist it and turn it till it only faintly resembles its former self. Bring along a camera, but if you forget, oh well—you've always got the memory.

Gorgeous snippets of memories from a friendship. There is dispute over who wrote this, John Lennon or Paul McCartney, although the latter is credited with it. It was recorded during very tense times in their own friendship. Matt Costa and Jack Johnson covered this one on their 2006 tour together.

HOW TO OVERCOME THE HARD TIMES: THE OBSTACLES

Sometimes it seems like life's obstacles—the hard times, the bad friends, the people who seemed good but let you down—are coming at you as fast as the spins in the last cycle of the washing machine. It may be comforting to know that these problems are common. Or it may not.

It's natural to be conflicted at times when we are figuring out who we are and what our place is in the world. That sort of soul-searching is going to produce a whole lot of extreme emotions and wild behavior. It's going to lead to people acting out and doing plain ol' dumb stuff.

Crud happens. Bad junk happens. Toxicity gets in the way. Lameness gets out of control. These are just facts of life. How you choose to handle the bad times is part of what defines you as a person and as a friend.

day sixteen
THE WAY-DOWN FRIEND

She is sinking fast.
You make for a quicksand grab;
Farther down she goes.

Do you have a friend who is really down? Most of us do. There are really two kinds of down, though. First there is the friend who is just going through a rough patch, who can normally handle life and its curveballs but who took an extra hardball to the gut recently and just needs some time to heal, whether from a breakup, a friendship issue or a family matter. And then there is the Downer friend with a capital "D." The one who is always negative, who complains incessantly and who always seems to be teetering on the edge of breakdown. Her problems could very well be chemical—she could have depression issues that you simply do not and cannot know about. Those girls need friends too, but if they are constantly sucking up all the air, how can you breathe?

This is some serious gray area. It simply isn't black-and-white, dump them or save them. (By the way, you can't save them, I was just using that as an example of an extreme.) You have to look inside yourself, call on your intuition and the gut feeling deep in the pit of your tummy and think: Has she *always* been like this? Or did something in her life really affect her so strongly that she's sinking? Because if she's always been like this, her depression may be too big for you to handle. She may need professional help. But if something sad or bad has caused her to retreat, time and friendship can surely heal her.

Ultimately, you have to call on your superfriend powers, the ones deep inside, to know if this person is draining you dry or if she simply needs a strong friend to help her out of the woods. I trust that on this, Day Sixteen, you've fine-tuned those abilities and have at least the start of an answer within.

ACTIVITY 16

How do you talk to a sad friend? Most of us would naturally say something along the lines of "You'll get through this." It's true, of course, but it sounds so trite. Not to mention, it never *feels* like you'll "get through this" at the time.

There is a way to talk to your gloomy chum in a manner that will not put her off and that can hopefully do her some real good. Start by acknowledging her pain. Do that by saying something like "I'm so sorry you're going through this." It sounds simple, but it's so much better than the cheery yet empty optimism of "You'll get through this."

Next, mobilize the troops. By that I mean gather your friends—the more, the better. They don't have to say anything or talk about the problem, they just have to be present and attentive. It lets her know that she has this support system standing by. It lets her know that there is good in life even if she doesn't see it at that moment. And it lets her know all that with nary a word spoken.

Finally, ask her for advice. It can be about anything. It shouldn't be obviously forced, like asking for advice on math homework when she clearly sucks at geometry. But asking for her opinion or her help reestablishes her self-worth. It makes her subtly realize that others count on her and her strengths, that other people need her.

These three steps won't cure what ails her. What they'll do is allow for some bonding when she needs it most.

SONG OF THE DAY:
FIONA APPLE, "SULLEN GIRL"
The quintessential Downer, capital D, has a pretty voice and biting lyrics but would probably be a really tough person to be friends with. Play this after a draining day with a friend to further empathize (vocabulary word!) with her and her plight.

Day Seventeen
THE QUEST FOR PERFECTION

Body, grades, friends, clothes.
Only the best will do—more!
Parties, boyfriends, stuff!

The Quest for Perfection is an impossible one. (*To dream the impossible dream . . .*) And yet as teens we strive to be perfect, often to the point of not being ourselves, and even worse, not liking ourselves.

IMPORTANT OBVIOUS FACT: No one is perfect.

Not even the girl you've seen from afar who has the perfect skin and the perfect body. I'd betcha twenty dollars and a choco milk shake that her life, in spite of her skin, is not perfect. Look around. All of the people you see are just that: people. And people have lives outside of your view. And in those lives they have challenges and difficulties and problems, because no one is immune to the challenges and difficulties of life.

Not Rihanna. Not Jessica Alba. Not Vanessa Hudgens and her perfect skin. No one. We simply do not know about everyone's thoughts and private lives.

IMPORTANT OBVIOUS FACT: Apparent physical perfection is not the equivalent of happiness.

When I was younger, I used to think, "If only my nose were just smaller, I would be so happy. Life would be so much better." Guess what? My face caught up with my nose—it ain't that big anymore—and that didn't change a damn thing. It wasn't till I was a little older that I realized that while my face isn't model-gorgeous, it suits me just fine.

Until as recently as a hundred years ago in China, small feet were considered desirable in women. Girls' feet were tightly bound so that they would not grow. The practice resulted in broken bones, deformed feet, infection and even paralysis, all in the name of tradition and style. Sounds crazy, right? But wanting plastic surgery to have your nose look like Natalie Portman's or your lips look like Angelina Jolie's isn't?

Our idiosyncrasies are what make us special. Those little off bits about us. You need to celebrate them, revel in them, enjoy them, for they are you.

As for the perfect grades or the perfect clothes—those things are fleeting. The joy will be momentary and then you're off to race for the next perfect moment. You will

rarely be satisfied. But if you stop and enjoy the process—
the act of trying hard, of studying and performing your
best—the high you get will be longer-lasting and, frankly,
more meaningful.

And the search for perfect friends? No such thing.
Even the most popular girls are not the perfect friends, because no one is that. You have to know that there will be
ups, there will be downs, there will be annoyances and
that's all okay. You can deal with it, provided everything
isn't coming at you a million miles an hour.

When we make mistakes, we learn. When we are
human together, when we share our mistakes and what
we've learned from them with others, our relationships
deepen. If things were perfect, you wouldn't learn. You can
succeed without perfection and you'll value yourself more.
There is always tomorrow.

ACTIVITY 17

Celebrate the dork in you with karaoke in your driveway.
There is no better way to dork out than to get a microphone
in hand and hit the street.

Don't have a karaoke machine? Rent one. Seriously,
you can, just Google it. If renting one is out of your price
range, then fake it. When I was a kid we would invite the
neighbor children over—the ones who were younger than
us, of course—put AC/DC's "Back in Black" on the
turntable and blast it. Then my brother and I would stand
inside, facing out the giant plate-glass window in the front
of our house. We grabbed our air guitars and sang along as

loud as we could. (We had to be heard through the window, natch.) Yeah, that's pretty old-school. But you can plug an MP3 player into an old boom box or bring your stereo out to the street with a really long extension cord.

So invite your friends over or just wait for passersby to take notice. Grab the mike. Dress up if you like in crazy outfits (this signals to the world that you are in fact doing this on purpose, and it begs the question "Don't it look like fun?").

SILLY SONGS TO SING

• Queen, "Fat Bottomed Girls," because methinks there has never been a more ridiculous song.

• The Weakerthans, "Plea from a Cat Named Virtute," because this song was written from the perspective of a cat!

• Anything by George Michael or Wham!

• And, of course, anything by AC/DC!

• For high cheese and lowbrow imperfection you can't lose with Whitney, Christina and Britney.

• For some silly indie-rock karaoke try Of Montreal's "Tim I Wish You Were Born a Girl" or Neutral Milk Hotel's "King of Carrot Flowers Pt. One."

• Rilo Kiley's "The Frug" because you can do the dance moves too.

- Nena's "99 Luftballons," just because!

- Anything by Madonna, the Donnas or Tegan and Sara.

- Songs by Cake or the Pixies are easy to sing and often very odd, in a good way.

- You simply cannot go wrong with show tunes!

- Add your own ideas of silly, ridiculous driveway karaoke tunes: _____
  _____
  _____
  _____
  _____

Do this and revel in the good life, the fun stuff, the happiness and joy you have with friends. It's so far from perfect, right? And yet it still feels so darn good.

SONG OF THE DAY:
CHRISTINA AGUILERA, "I TURN TO YOU"
If you say bad karaoke, I say Christina! This isn't just a friendship song, this is a friendship *anthem*. I don't care if you hate on her, you got to love this song and its over-the-top friendship-love.

DAY EIGHTEEN
PRESSURE COOKER

Note: "yes" rhymes with "stress."
Have you thought about that one?
I'm not your puppet.

Peer pressure is like the after-school-special topic of the century. Everyone has been lectured on it, told to avoid it, to *just say no*. But let's face it: most of us succumb at one point or another. I want to share with you a little nugget of now-obvious information that changed my way of thinking on the whole subject. It all comes down to choice.

The way I see it, you don't just have the right to make choices (for instance, to say no to people pressuring you). You have a *responsibility* to make choices, because that is what your life is—it's the choices you make. And that is ultimately the crux of peer pressure:

"Am I going to make a choice for myself or am I going to let someone else make it for me?"

When you do let others choose for you, you're straight-up giving up your choice. Forfeiting it. You know in your gut when you shouldn't do something. That's your intuition talking and your common sense acting up. Listen to them. Don't be afraid or embarrassed by not going along with others, because, bottom line—this is *your* life and *you* are the only person who will have to answer for it.

I remember feeling like I had no control when I was younger—I felt like my parents completely ran my life. I was straining at every corner to make my own decisions. Most everyone has felt this way at least once. But listen, this is your shot. This is your time to make those choices and exercise your control. You actually get to make decisions for yourself all the time; you just don't always look at these moments exactly that way.

So think for yourself and value your own ability. If you respect your responsibility to do so, saying no becomes a whole lot easier.

Oh, and one more thing: everyone is so *not* doing it.

ACTIVITY 18

It's not so much an activity today as it is a flat-out lesson in how to say no to people. It's an important skill that you will be able to use your entire life. When you get older peer pressure can take on altogether new forms at work ("Just take this project off my hands"), with friends ("I need to borrow five hundred dollars") or in family life ("We really need your expertise as chair of the mother-daughter fashion show"). Ew.

I know it's hard when you're faced with a spur-of-the-moment question—there seems to be just a split-second to make the choice. But in reality, there is more time. And you need to take at least a moment to think about the consequences of what you're agreeing to. What could happen if you say *yes* to something you feel isn't quite right? Once you've given any situation some legitimate thought and carried it through to the potential end-scenarios, it becomes a whole lot clearer.

There are really a whole lot of ways to say no. Here are some I'm rather fond of.

The Crazy No

Laugh off the suggestion as ludicrous. "You crack me up, what a hilarious thought!" Note: you didn't even utter the word "no" and yet you still got the sentiment across.

The More-Options No

Come up with a better idea. "No thanks . . . but we could do this: ―――――――――――."

The Concerned No

Make it sound like you're looking out for the others. "Hey, I don't want you to get in trouble."

The Polite No

You've got to muster up the confidence for this one, because it needs to be said with great authority. It consists of a simple and direct "No thank you."

The Excuse No

Now is your chance to give a reason for the no. It can be honest or it can be slightly exaggerated for comic effect.

The Praise No

"You always have the best ideas, but I just can't." By complimenting the person first, you're slyly getting out of the situation with a touch of grace.

The Change-the-Subject No

"No, I can't go out with you tomorrow—hey, did you finish that geometry assignment?" Bonus points for phrasing the new subject in the form of a question.

The Team No

It's always easier if you can say no with another person by your side. Strength in numbers, baby.

The Quick No

This one is good if you're feeling a little scared and/or embarrassed. Say it quick and get the heck out of Dodge.

SONG OF THE DAY:
YEAH YEAH YEAHS, "NO NO NO"

The last way to say no is in a song. Just blast this one in their faces. They should get the hint. Who wouldn't—what with Karen O wailing like a wounded dog, "No, no, no . . ."

DAY NINETEEN
SAVE THE DRAMA FOR YOUR MAMA

An evil disease
In your pores, under your nails—
Can you stop the talk?

It's somewhat accepted, isn't it? Like a guilty pleasure, or an annoying but excusable bad habit. There are zillions of Web sites and blogs devoted to it. I admit it. I read them.

But is gossip excusable? Is it just a bad habit like biting your nails? Finger chomping doesn't hurt anyone but yourself, but talking trash hurts a whole lot of people. It does, so don't roll your eyes. Words don't break bones like those sticks and those stones, but they sure bruise the big stuff like ego, self-esteem and confidence.

We gossip because it makes us feel special, like a member of some secret club, and because, frankly, when we put others down it can somehow make us feel elevated ourselves—we feel like we are "better." But in reality it does no such thing. In reality gossipers are always looked down upon as untrustworthy. (Not a quality we're looking for in a friend, mind you.) All these bloggers who've become faux celebs themselves by trashing others on their admittedly oft-witty Web sites aren't looked at with respect and admiration. They're thought of as snakes—funny snakes, but snakes just the same. Talking smack reflects on you as much as it does on the person you're talking trash about.

What's heartbreaking is that a lot of girls gossip about their own friends. Maybe they don't use the word "gossip." But they speak unfavorably about friends to the others in their group. They are catty. This sours everything. How does it make the talked-about person feel? And what about the listener? Participating in catty gossip chatter makes you feel kind of dirty, doesn't it? Plus, it straight-up weakens friendships.

POINT: It is absolutely considered gossip if the person you're speaking of were to walk up and hear you and feel embarrassed and/or mortified.

"Karen has such great shoes." = Not gossip.

"I heard Suzie tell Karen it looks like Karen got her shoes off the bag lady on Forty-seventh Street." = Gossip!

Have you ever thought about how tiring it is to be caustic and snarky all the time? Gossip is pretty much a complete waste of energy and time. Seriously, what comes of it? What good in the world happens due to gossip? Nothing. It's a time waster. The only thing gossip does is hurt someone or make someone angry. And maybe somebody gets a chuckle or two (at someone else's expense). But isn't that what cable television is for?

So how do you control gossip, stop it in your circle of friends? You talk about it.

Talk about the benefits (none) of continuing. And make a concerted effort to curb it. What if they don't wanna stop? You've got to ask yourself if you truly want a friend who is unabashedly mean and negative. *You* can refuse to listen, *you* can refuse to spread it. *You* can politely tell the offender that it just ain't cool to say those things when the other person's not around. Your actions do speak louder than your words. By refusing to participate, you're setting others up to follow your good example, you groovy Girl Scout, you.

And Another Thing . . .

You know what else smells like gossip, tastes like gossip and hurts like gossip? Excluding people. Other girls, other friends. It's totally natural to think that to get closer to one person you have to push others away, but it doesn't actually work like that. When we exclude other girlfriends from things like sleepovers or lunch tables, when we're secretive and tell "inside" jokes and stories, we're being mean. We're not being good friends. And just because it's not aimed at your BFF doesn't make it all right. You're not exhibiting good friend behavior, and that, in fact, colors *all* your friendships.

ACTIVITY 19

Save the drama for your mama and save the gossip for a short story. Seriously, gossiping is, in part, storytelling. Why not channel that positive aspect of a negative activity into something wholly creative? You probably know what writing prompts are from school, but essentially, the following sentences should serve as the first sentence to your story or the inspiration for it. You can get a little caustic here if you like, just don't use real names of real people in real situations. Go ahead and put someone you know in a ridiculous scenario if you're doing this just for your own reading pleasure. In other words, don't even use real names if you plan to share this at school or with friends. Choose one or two of these prompts and get writing.

- Take two people who dislike each other and stick them on a plane in adjacent seats. Now what happens?
- You wake up, go to the sink, look in the mirror and whoa! You don't see *you* looking back at you, you see the face of someone you don't like. Begin your story.
- Use these words in one short story: "friend," "ring," "destructive," "marshmallow" and "wonderful."
- Start a story with "I used to think . . ."
- Start a story with "They had nothing to say to one another, and yet . . . "
- Recall a time when you did something to get noticed. Write about it.
- Write about a difficult decision you've had to make recently.
- You get three wishes—now write about your choices.

FRIENDSHIP IS *NOT* A COMPETITIVE SPORT

Gaggles of girlfriends,
A parade of perky pals—
This is the life, right?

I have always hung in a group. Sure, there was usually someone in the group who I was especially close to, but I have been part of a pack of girls as long as I can remember. The pros are obvious—a huge support group, multitudes of friends to call on when you're bored, hungry, in need, feeling the friendship love and want to just plain hang out.

But the cons? There is often a whole competitive jockey-for-power thing going on in these groups, and that can inspire neg words and feelings as opposed to the pro posi stuff.

I've watched ex-friends who've undermined their best

girlfriends' relationships with boys because they felt *they* weren't getting enough attention. But life ain't a competition and it ain't a reality show. When you treat it as such, you get into head-to-head battles with those around you, including your friends. And frankly, that makes you no friend at all. Plus, it just isn't fun.

To feel worthy, some girls have to be the best or have the most stuff or be the loudest or hold all the power in a relationship. But it's so much more rewarding to be there for your friends, to be a good friend to someone else, than it is to win something. The glory of winning one battle is short-lived. It's over and then you are off in search of a new battle. This search can be constant and you won't ever feel satisfied. But being a good friend feels good long-term.

You should never judge your own worth or successfulness by others' successes. Your friends' successes do not lessen yours.

Every girl will have her moments to shine. Let her do so. When it's another friend's turn, shine the spotlight brightly on her, don't try to hog it. And then when it's your turn, it will really be *your* turn.

When you're the one feeling like a third (or seventh) wheel, it's time to regroup. Look around and make sure that there isn't a legitimate reason you're not being included, like your friends happen to be going to a volleyball party and you're not on the team. Is there someone else feeling out in the cold who you can find common ground with? Evaluate—are these your real friends? If so, make an effort (you'll find *muchos* examples inside this book). If not, it may be time to hit the first section of this here tome and be on the lookout for new friends. Most important of all, though, is taking the time to be by yourself and think about what you want in a friend. You've learned a lot these last twenty days. Use those lessons and really examine the people around you. Make sure you're taking time for *you*, for making yourself happy. Exercise (it doesn't have to be on some boring treadmill— go for a hike or swim), listen to music that makes you feel alive, get some sunshine or take in a funny movie or read a hilarious book. You have to take care of yourself and be happy by yourself to be happy as a part of any group.

I'm still friends with my group of girls from days gone by, even though we've moved away from one another. The supercompetitive girls have fallen by the wayside, and what remains is a group of girls who are supportive, genuine, loving and fun. We still e-mail and talk on the phone. And every year we get together and rent a house for a long weekend and eat, hike, swim, read trashy magazines and laugh our bums off. As soon as it's over, we're all looking forward to the next year.

ACTIVITY 20

Gather a gaggle of girlfriends to engage in the most noncompetitive "sport" there is: yoga. But none of that chakra crystal life-force vitality mumbo jumbo today. We're gonna do it indie-rock style.

Invite your group of girls over and tell them to come in sweats and tees. No fancy workout duds, please. Nothing matchy-matchy. They can bring yoga mats or towels.

Beforehand, hit the library and pick up a yoga DVD— nothing too hard. If there are choices, look for something more power yoga-ish. That will get you sweating and limber. Once you're home, scan it and check out how long the warm-up, the actual workout and then the cooldown are. Take note, because now it's time to make the playlist. You can download it to an iPod, burn a CD or just cue up some CDs you'll play like a DJ.

SOME SUGGESTIONS FOR WARM-UP MUSIC
- Joan as Police Woman, "The Ride"
- Regina Spektor, "Oedipus"
- The Softlightes, "Untitled Duet #3"
- José González, "Heartbeats"
- Zero 7, "Destiny"

SOME SUGGESTIONS FOR WORKOUT MUSIC
- Iron & Wine, "Boy with a Coin"
- Sea Wolf, "You're a Wolf"
- Au Revoir Simone, "The Lucky One"
- Sarah McLachlan, "Dirty Little Secret" (Thievery Corporation Mix)
- The Postmarks, "Goodbye"
- Beth Orton, "Carmella"
- Tegan and Sara, "Walking with a Ghost"

SOME SUGGESTIONS FOR COOLDOWN MUSIC
- Anything by My Morning Jacket, The Album Leaf, Hum, The Innocence Mission or Charlotte Gainsbourg

OTHER GOOD INDIE-ROCK YOGA MUSIC:

_____

_____

_____

_____

_____

_____

_____

Clear away the furniture so that there is room for you all to spread out on your mats in front of the TV. When your friends arrive, cue up the video but turn the volume way down—all those videos have chiming bells and sitar music, and that is not what we are going for today. Then turn on *your* music and do the downward dog. . . .

SONG OF THE DAY:
JILL CUNNIFF, "HAPPY WARRIORS"
This former Luscious Jackson member spins a fun dance tune about getting together with the girls and making the best of life, together. Invite your pals to stick around after yoga and have an impromptu dance party.

day twenty-one
PARENTAL PAIN

Do your folks want you
Locked away forever and ever?
Really? So doubtful.

When our parents dislike one or more of our friends, it sure can make life more difficult.

I'd like you to stop for a moment and really think this one through: do you honestly think your parents set rules and express an interest in who you hang out with to annoy you? Are they doing it to be evil? Or mean? Or even controlling? Not likely.

Probably they are concerned because they care about you, worry about you, want (what they think is) the best for you. They want to know where you're going so that they know where to find you if something happens. And likewise, they want to know who you are with so that they know who to contact if they ever need to. But what about when they don't like your friends?

Since we've established that they probably aren't doing this out of some malevolent dastardly plan, let's just for a quiet moment give them the benefit of the doubt and think about *why* they wouldn't like one of your friends. Because they might be on to something (or not). I mean, there may be a valid reason (or not). But you need to really think about it.

Sometimes a parent—or another observer—can see something in someone that you can't when you're smack in the middle of the friendship. And since your folks have your best interests at heart, I think it's worth a consideration, a real honest-to-goodness look-see as to why they feel this way. Perhaps their fears are unfounded, and in that case, your friend can make an attempt to get in their good graces. But maybe your parents are right and you'll learn something from them. Oh, the horror!

Sometimes the problem can be boiled down to miscommunication. For instance, your parents could be passing judgment or making an assumption based on the clothes your friend wears. Or perhaps they're put off because your friend has a way different set of rules than your parents have set for you. These kinds of issues can likely be worked out through communication. Other issues may not be so easily fixed. If you consistently get into trouble with a particular friend, do you think your parents have reason to worry?

It can go the other way too. What if you're a parentally unliked friend? Can you ask yourself why? Does the parent have a reason? Do you need to atone for some heinous crime? Or do you just need to be friendlier and make more of an effort? Most parents aren't looking for kids who are overly sweet—it makes them suspicious and doesn't seem genuine. Gifts aren't necessary, unless they're having you over for dinner, and then something small could be nice. Really, the key is to talk. Seriously. So many young people get around adults and they clam up and don't know what to say. This too makes some parents understandably nervous. If you answer questions and ask some yourselves ("Oh, do you play chess?" "The house smells good, what is that?"), parents will see that you are respectful, intelligent and friendly. And those are the qualities parents are looking for when shopping for friends for their children.

●●●●●●●●●●●●●●●●●●●●●●●●●●●●●●●

ACTIVITY 21

At the heart of this issue is communication with your parents. It's so easy to come in and out of their lives, their houses, without saying much these days. You've got to know, this tends to make folks jittery. Less talk means more suspicion! More talk leads to greater trust!

So today's activity involves communicating with your folks. When you learn more about them, and vice versa, there is simply a better understanding between you. You'll all be reminded that no one is operating in a vacuum— there are circumstances that have led you all to your beliefs and feelings and ways of life. So today I say, interview your parents. I'll get you started with some questions about their past and present, but I bet you have some of your own.

- Where were you born? Where was your mother born? Your father?
- Did your mom have any special talents?
- Can you tell me about any "black sheep" in the family?
- Are there stories about famous or infamous relatives on either side of the family?
- Has anybody in the family ever had any unusual psychic abilities?
- Do you know the story of how your parents met and fell in love?
- What was your favorite meal when you were young?
- What were your favorite books when you were a kid?
- How do you think you are like your mother? Your father?
- Did your mom ever lose her temper? Over what? What about your dad?
- Did your parents have good senses of humor?
- What is the saddest event you can remember?
- What world events had an impact on your life when you were growing up?
- What do you think is the key to a successful marriage?
- What has been your proudest moment as a parent?
- If you could have worked in another profession, what would it have been?
- What accomplishments are you most proud of?
- What is the one thing you want people to remember about you?

In return, let them ask questions of you. And here's the rough part—actually answer them. With more-than-one-word answers! The more you communicate with your parents, the more they will respect and trust you.

DAY TWENTY-TWO
FRENEMIES

Friends should not be mean
Or cut you down to pieces.
Oh, with friends like these . . .

Not all friendships are meant to be. Perhaps there is a chemical imbalance in the air when the two of you get together. Maybe it's her, maybe it's you, but bottom line is that not everyone is meant to be your BFF.

A frenemy, obviously derived from "friend" and "enemy," is that girl who throws backstabbing comments and backhanded compliments your way. Her cut-downs are cloaked in perfume and therefore don't smell as funky—at first. Her advice is dispensed with an air of superiority, and she's the first one to remind you of your lowest moments when you're feeling good. These are not things friends do.

Usually we have a love-hate relationship with these toxic girls, but the love isn't so much love as it is an odd admiration, and the hate is usually more envy than anything else. Frenemies fuel our insecurities, which then fuel our own weird ass-backward idolatry.

Why do we put up with our frenemies? Usually out of fear. We're often scared of what a frenemy will do or say if we cross her. We're scared of being left out or left behind somehow. We also might think it's easier to deal with her than to face the idea of losing her. It's all a bit twisted.

Remember, it doesn't have to be like this. You don't deserve someone who treats you as less-than. There are plenty of other girls out there, plenty of other friendships to forge.

But if you want to hold on to this friendship, then focus on the good stuff about this gal. Avoid situations that your friend will not shine in; don't tell her the things you know she won't support you on. She doesn't have to be the friend you go to with everything—she can be a midlevel: more than an acquaintance, less than a BFF. That's okay.

Finally, don't let her shenanigans get to you. This is gonna sound like something your mom would say, but really, it's *her* problem—she's doing this because of some insecurity or deficiency in her own life. Don't sink to her level and dish it back at her. Enjoy her for who she is and focus on her best qualities. Or walk away. Once again, you've got a choice. It's pretty much all up to you.

ACTIVITY 22

Focus today on a friend who is *not* toxic, who would *never* fall into the frenemy category. Push aside those girls, at least for the day, and give your full attention to a friend who is the opposite of all that is noxious. I'm talking about the friend who says all the right things, who makes you feel like you can conquer the world. She may not be your closest friend right now. She may not be the one you spend the most time with or see every day. But when you're together, you feel flipping good.

Today, make her something personal and special. It could be anything, but my suggestion is inexpensive, fun and meaningful. It's personalized stationery.

Pick up about *ten or fifteen sheets of some pretty yet fairly plain paper.* Any size will do, but something a bit out of the ordinary would be best—square or extrasmall or thin and long. Pick up *some envelopes* as well, some that aren't matchy-matchy but are contrasting and cool paired up with the paper. And dig out an *old rubber-stamp set* if you have one; otherwise pick one up at the art store. Initials are way easy and obviously just-for-her special. But you can also think about things that mean a lot to her and see if you can't find something that relates to that. You can even—and honestly, this is the coolest option yet—get a rubber stamp made. Look up "rubber stamps" in the phone book and I'd bet money that you'll find a few places that do custom stamps. You give them your artwork and twenty-four hours later they've turned it into a stamp—it usually costs between $10 and $20. After you stamp the paper and turn it into stationery, you can wrap the stamp up and gift it along with the paper as part of the present.

TO MAKE THE STATIONERY

• Dip the stamp in an ink pad and press it on the top center of the paper or around the borders, and let it dry.

• Don't forget to use one of the pieces to write her a note, just letting her know you were thinking of her and you wanted to thank her for being a part of your life. It doesn't have to be a sobby sentiment. Say it from your heart, and if that means just saying "Hey, you rock!" then that's what it should say.

• Finally, wrap it all up and put some sort of bow on it to tie it all together. I don't know why, but bows just make it all more special somehow.

SONG OF THE DAY:
PULP, "LIKE A FRIEND"
This is the quiet, sad story of the ultimate frenemy. I love that it's called "Like a Friend," because on some levels this person is acting like friends, but on the most important levels he is doing exactly the opposite.

Day Twenty-Three
THE BOYFRIEND STEALER

He is my dream guy—
He is so not right for her.
Lame old excuses . . .

There are a couple of reasons girls like to pursue guys who are already in relationships. The first is that it's often easier to get to know a guy when there are no expectations. In other words, if you think he's off the market yet cute, it's probably easier to talk to him than if he's just cute. I'm not making excuses, I simply think this is how it sometimes happens.

The second reason is a bit more sinister. Some gals like to go for taken boys because it makes them feel powerful. It makes them feel better than someone else if they can make a guy dump his girlfriend. It falsely and arrogantly raises their self-esteem.

Neither of the aforementioned reasons is okay, because if you mess around with another girl's guy you're being deceitful, disrespectful and—oh yeah—a horrible friend.

The girl who engages in this behavior should not be trusted. Not because of what she's doing with the boy, but because of what she's doing to her friend's heart.

Don't fall into the trap that says "But he's the one for me, he's perfect for *me*—not *her*." Phooey. News flash: There is no such thing as "the one." There are multiple "ones," and the trick is finding one of them when the timing is right. If that one has a girlfriend, the timing is wrong. So if you miss an opportunity with him, there will be another opportunity around the bend.

I haven't always been the perfect friend or the perfect person. I've done some stupid, stupid stuff in my life. But I can unequivocally say there is one thing I've never done: gone after another girl's guy. Period.

When Your BFF Has a New Boy in Her Life

This is the very common occurrence wherein one good friend becomes part of a new love-y couple and proceeds to spend all her time with the new boy and no time with the old friend(s). Here's how you deal— you start by talking to your pal about it. There is a real possibility that your girlfriend doesn't even realize she's doing it. Let her know you miss her. Maybe she will see the error of her ways. And cut her a bit of slack, particularly if the whole world of relationships is brand-new to her. I'm not saying you should just let it slide—I still think you should talk it out— but know that the newness of it all will pass, and it's quite likely that in a few weeks' time she'll be back to her friend-centric self. Try to be understanding, and don't let any jealousy tinge your "I just miss her" sadness with "why can't it be me?" anger. And if you yourself have fallen victim to the charms of a new romantic relationship and neglected your ol' pals, think about your actions. It's fun to be with the new guy, but don't take your friends for granted. Make sure you still make time for those mega-important relationships—i.e., your friendships—too.

ACTIVITY 23

There are basic laws of friendship that you should abide by. I informally refer to them as the Girl Code. At the heart of the Girl Code is this basic premise: treat your girlfriends with respect.

This is my own version of the Girl Code. Don't use it to manipulate your friends; use it for good only. Feel free to write it out in calligraphy on a piece of parchment paper, spray-paint it on your walls (get some approval on that one) or cross-stitch it on a pillow. Your choice.

THE GIRL CODE

1. When our girlfriends are down, we lift them up. And we do so with honest-to-goodness sincerity.
2. We do not speak poorly of our friends behind their backs, particularly to mutual friends. Nor do we conspire with friends in any way to undermine other girls.
3. We recognize that crushes are powerful but fleeting. We do not allow our crushes on boys to interfere with our friendships.
4. As girlfriends we do not go after our friends' boyfriends, ex-boyfriends and (with a few exceptions) brothers. This goes for flirting, too. N-O.
5. We do not fight with girls over boys—not mentally, emotionally or, dare we say it, physically.
6. We do not ask our girlfriends to lie for us or put them in awkward or compromising positions. If we choose to do these things for our friends, so be it, but we never manipulate or coerce our girlfriends.
7. Straight up, we keep the private stuff private.

And Another Thing . . .

I recall only one time in my past when a boy got between a girlfriend and me. I spotted this cute boy at a coffee shop and not two days later saw him again, but this time he was with someone I knew. I spoke with them and reported back to my pal Michelle that I had met him and he was even foxier up close. The next week Michelle ran into him with our mutual friend and thought he was as dreamy as I did. She announced that she was gonna give it a crack, since he and I hadn't had anything more than a brief conversation. I was crushed. *"Saw him first!"* I screamed to no one but myself. In her defense, I didn't have any claim to him, and for all we knew, he didn't like short girls (me) and adored blondes (her). A query to his friend revealed that he thought us both "cute." But her height and blondness were still factors, and I quickly grew bitter. Feeling the sting of a future rejection, I backed out of this unwanted race. In this case my LMO served me fine. (LMO? Lameus modus operandi, wherein I cut my losses rather than take a risk—but risks in life, and in friendship, provide bounties of goodness.) Michelle went on a date with him that was neither exciting nor interesting, a date that ended in the single worst kiss of her life: sloppy, dripping wet, slightly stinky and awkwardly unpleasant. In the end, she declared me the victor.

We don't always come to these conclusions in the neatest, nicest ways, but we get there eventually.

A boy never, ever came between us again. I can't even remember that guy's name! But Michelle is still a huge part of my life.

HOW TO ACHIEVE THAT
SECOND "F" IN "BFF":
THE FOREVER FRIEND

There are friends and then there are Friends. A Friend is the girl who you connect with, who makes you feel brilliant and you do the same for her.

You may be ready for that, want that, need that. But you can't force it. If it's meant to be, if you two really connect, then you can help it along by focusing on a few major components of the profound Forever Friendship.

These are the things that bond us permanently to others. They once again come from the wellspring that is your choice—when you choose to be present and connect, that signals the bells and whistles and fireworks. The fact is, you could choose not to do these things. And that's why choosing to be a great friend is so valuable. It's an act of will.

Now, listen, if you are also trying to nurture four other friendships to BFF status, well, good luck. It likely won't work. Becoming really close with someone takes focus and time. You've got to *team up* with the person, not just hang out.

But that's a joy, ain't it?

DAY TWENTY-FOUR
X FACTOR

In my book, you'd win
The whole thing—confetti,
Balloons, the title.

You probably haven't thought about your friends in this way, but here and now, give it a try. Pick a friend and think about that special source of pride you have in her. As Simon Cowell would say on *American Idol*, it's that X factor. It's the thing she is good at, but sometimes it's even more— it's a quality in her you admire and respect.

For instance, my friend Karen is extremely organized, something of which I am in awe because I am extremely *un*organized. She also has this wonderfully positive attitude toward life. I am truly confident that with those two qualities so firmly in hand, my friend can do anything she sets her mind to.

My pal Amy is a creative genius and a real artist, and when you combine that with her warmth and intelligence, well, she's a force to be reckoned with.

And my own X factor? Well, I think it's my drive to keep going. I have a ton of ideas, more than can fit in my head, and I'm a risk taker (not to be confused with physical risk taking à la bungee jumping—I would *never*). But when it comes to my dreams, I go after them.

Besides making you feel singsong good, this is another obvious benefit to having someone believe in you. When I don't have the confidence to go on, when I am feeling mega-low, both Amy and Karen have stepped in as my temporary surrogate confidence. And it's more than empty talk. Their real-life belief in me puffs me up with possibilities. Their pep talks are never empty or generic. They zero in on my X factor and remind me of why I am worthy. I know at those moments that my friends believe in me enough to get me over this hurdle and on to the next chapter of my life.

ACTIVITY 24

This activity is about appreciating your friends' best qualities; it's about recognizing them and thanking the moon and the stars that your friends have come into your life.

We're going to start by crafting our own envelope. You will need an *envelope* (used is fine) that you are going to undo the seams of to make a template. You'll need *paper for your new homemade envelope.* Provided the original envelope isn't too big, you can use a page from a magazine. Pick something meaningful to the friend you are recognizing.

Once you've opened the seams of the envelope, lay it out flat on the magazine page or other colorful paper. Trace around the edges carefully with a pencil, then use scissors to cut out the shape. Once again place the original flattened envelope on top of the now cut-out piece. Use it as a guide to see where to fold the seams—refold the original envelope, taking the new one along for the ride.

Remove the old envelope from the equation (and save for future envelope making), take a glue stick and apply to the side folds so that they stick. Do not yet put any glue on the top "lick 'em" flap.

Now cut up some small fortune cookie–size strips of paper, and on them write down those things that comprise your friend's X factor, one per each strip of paper. Start each sentence with "I'm proud of your_____ " or "You can do anything you want because of your _____ " or even "Your X factor is _____ ." Slip some into the envelope and then seal the top flap with either more glue stick or a secure sticker. And then mail it to your friend.

You heard me, mail it. Even if she lives next door. Mail it. Because who doesn't love mail? We all do!

To mail these sorts of envelopes you're gonna need to make a space for your pal's address. Put a white sticker on the front and write directly on that, or print out her address on white paper and cut it out and glue that on the front. If the print or picture is light enough, you can even write the address boldly on the front with a Sharpie and it will get there—it just may take an extra day or two. (Because it will have to be hand-sorted. Those postal machines can't read words on backgrounds.)

SONG OF THE DAY:
OLD 97s, "FRIENDS FOREVER"
A song about finding a way to stay close to the friends from school who like you for who you really are and the star power you have hiding within.

DAY TWENTY-FIVE
AN ASTUTE AMIGO

There is a whole world
Waiting for you to explore.
Knowledge is power.

There are studies done by scientists—real ones—and they say that if you hang out with smarter people, you become smarter. And the converse is true—hang out with people doing dumb junk and you'll probably end up doing dumb junk too. But we don't need any study to tell us that, do we?

Your friends, of course, should support you and be kind, but there is another aspect of friendship that doesn't get talked about. Not all your friends are going to recognize this aspect, but a special one or two might. These friends can challenge you. Not to a duel or anything. Not in a confrontational manner. But they can challenge you to think bigger and broader about life than before. They can challenge you intellectually. They do so by engaging you in conversation about things you wouldn't ordinarily talk about, or things you simply don't talk about. It could be something personal like your dreams and goals or it could be something larger like politics and our place in the world.

I'll go ahead and beg this once: please take an active role in educating yourself. Even if school doesn't thrill you all the time, the outside world should. It's filled to the brim with different cultures, different perspectives and opinions, different sorts of people doing different sorts of things. The more you talk about the world and what's going on in it, the more educated you become about it. The more educated you are about the world, the more you have to talk about. The more you have to talk about, the more you have to share . . . with other people.

●●●●●●●●●●●●●●●●●●●●●●●●●●●●●●

ACTIVITY 25

Here's something to ponder and discuss: what part of your life do you think is not affected by politics? I suspect most of you would say the majority of your life is not. You'd answer things like your clothes, your food, your cell phone and your computer—the things that matter to you right here, right now.

But the government regulates how clothes are made; they control the production and cost of food as well as pesticides. The Federal Communications Commission (FCC) regulates all communication methods. Politics affects the smallest details of even *your* life. The government decides what is taught in public schools, where the money goes. Tax money pays for libraries, firefighters, police, roadwork and on and on and on. And here's an interesting—and yes, related—fact: if all the young women between the ages of eighteen and twenty-four in this country vote, they could decide who the next president is.

So today, your activity is to grab a friend and do a little research and then discuss.

Talk with your friend and decide on a country, a politician and a world issue that you've heard of. And then research them online. Read about the people of the country and what the capital city is like. Read about the voting record of your chosen politician. Investigate the background on a world issue, like poverty or the environment. Print some stuff out if you want. But together, dig deep.

Then go get a decaf mocha or some tea or just go for a walk-and-talk, but start actively engaging your brain about something new to you. You'll have more to talk about, more to think about, more to share.

Countries I'm Interested in:

_____

_____

_____

_____

_____

_____

_____

Important People I'm Interested in:

_____

_____

_____

_____

_____

_____

World Issues I'm Interested in:

_____

_____

_____

_____

_____

Web sites you can start at:

- YouThink.WorldBank.org gives you background on most of the world's issues, from the environment to health matters to globalization.

- Student-Voices.org is an online discussion and resource for national politics.

- Exploratorium.edu/origins takes you on virtual field trips to places of note around the world.

- Newseum.org collects newspapers from around the world that you can read online.

- DiscussionDivas.com is a free service you can sign up for. They will deliver a news story, and the background on said story, to your e-mail in-box once a week.

SONG OF THE DAY:
RILO KILEY, "IT'S A HIT"
You can also discuss the politics swimming around in this song from perhaps my second-favorite band of all time. Jenny Lewis makes some mighty bold statements about government in this tune. Do you agree? Disagree? Discuss.

DAY TWENTY-SIX
IT'S THE HARDEST WORD

I'm really very—
Sor, sor, sor, sor, sorry—if
You think I should be.

As Elton John sang in the seventies, "Sorry seems to be the hardest word."

Here's the real dirt. We will all experience moments of poor judgment in our lifetime. We will do or say something we shouldn't, or let someone down in some way, and that is life. It's normal. It's real. One infraction does not have to ruin a friendship. That is, if you can realize it warrants an apology and then deliver one.

Apologies are tricky. Most people don't want to revisit their poor behavior, so it's easier to pretend it did not happen or, worse, rewrite history so that they did nothing wrong. That's annoying, to say the least.

I had a friend who really put me in an uncomfortable position—she straight-up asked me to lie to our other friends to save her from embarrassment. I might have done it had it not made an innocent person look the fool. But she went ahead and told the lies anyway, even though I said I wouldn't back her up. We naturally went through a rough patch after that. But I didn't want to walk away from our friendship—I just wanted her to realize the position she'd put me (and the innocent party) in. A month later, she still wouldn't acknowledge any bad choices—or lies. In her version I had let her down as a friend for not backing her up. In her version not only had she not asked me to lie, but she also said she hadn't lied. She rewrote history to suit her own needs. That was the easy way out. Needless to say, that was the end of our friendship.

I can think of times I held on stubbornly to the idea that I didn't need to apologize, only to later gain some distance and perspective and realize I absolutely should have said I was sorry. It's hard to go back and correct those mistakes. But you can. It usually doesn't take much more than a genuine "Sorry." But saying you're sorry takes real effort and care.

"Sorry" shouldn't be used like a get-out-of-jail-free card. You can't be mean or cruel or hurtful just because you know you can always pull out the "sorry" and make it all better. That's lame.

But if you can effectively learn to say you're sorry, you can probably save a few friendships in your future that are worth holding on to. It's okay. We make mistakes. The key is owning up to them and moving on with few regrets.

WHAT IF you really and truly don't feel like an apology to a friend is warranted but you still want to try to get over this hurdle? I feel that the best way to do this is not to ignore the problem, but rather to go talk to said friend with soft eyes and a gentle voice and tell her, "I want us to get over this." And then ask her, "How do you think we can do that?" Make sure you have some ideas on how to get over it as well.

ACTIVITY 26

There are a handful of important steps to making an effective apology. Today we're going to learn the Art of Saying "Sorry." And it *is* an art. Like any art, it takes skill, discipline and attention to detail.

- Be Specific: Don't ever say "I'm sorry for whatever it is you think I did" or make any other generic apology that implies you aren't really sorry. That's like saying "I'm sorry if I hurt you." No " if 's" allowed! Tell your friend exactly what you are sorry for. This lets her know you are genuine.

- Take Responsibility: Don't pass the blame off and don't give excuses. Sorry saying is not the time for that. Using the word "I" when you apologize goes a long way; it says *you're* taking responsibility. "I know what I did was wrong."

- Show That You Get It: Think about how you'd feel if the tables were turned. How would you deal if she did what you did? That will help you understand how she's truly feeling. Practice your empathy!

- Explain: This is tricky, because it could come off as an excuse. Dig deep and think about the real reason you did what you did. If it's honest—and brief—you can probably give a teeny explanation, but this is a very small part of the apology, and if one part is to be skipped, this is it. It isn't about you feeling better right now. It's about your friend feeling better.

- Give Her the Love: This is where you remind her how important she is to you. Tell her exactly why. Hopefully this will trigger something in her mind that recalls the good in you.

- Make a Promise: Vow never to do this thing again. And really mean it. You can also ask her, "How can I make this up to you?" because maybe there is something specific she is looking for. Plus it puts the ball back in her court.

Finally, be patient. Sometimes even the most heartfelt apologies need time to soak in. So wait and see how your friend reacts down the road. Remember, it could be awkward for a bit afterward, even if she does forgive you. But odds are in your favor that with a bona fide twenty-four-karat apology, things will be better than ever in time.

SONG OF THE DAY:
JEM, "THEY"
With the high-pitched chorus of "I'm sorry, so sorry" floating about, you could play this tune in the background while you apologize. Or, you can just add this one to the friendship mix CD you'll give your friend after she forgives you.

DAY TWENTY-SEVEN
COSMOPOLITAN COMRADES

Hit the road with friends—
Trains, planes and automobiles,
Or simply your mind.

Did you know there are over fifty-seven million square miles of land on this planet? How much have you seen?

Of course, it's not always possible to travel, even if you want to get out and see the world. But that doesn't mean you and your friends have to live within a ten-block radius of your house. You can explore the world through books, the Internet, pen pals and friends.

Once you understand how vast the world is, something changes inside your body. You'll find you have more openness to new things, other cultures and new people. Do you now see where I am going with this?

The more of the world you see and explore, the more people you will meet, the more friends you will make. But there is also an aura that you will cultivate around yourself—that of the cosmopolitan girl who has seen the world and understands her important place in it.

By exploring with a friend, whether it be backpacking through Europe or doing the activity below, which doesn't involve any frequent-flier miles at all, you'll grow closer, more intertwined in each other's evolution. And being part of each other's growth is exactly the sort of thing that triggers those inner-soul-sister friendship feelings.

ACTIVITY 27

It's time to plan a trip with your girlfriend. Don't tell me it will never happen. Part of the journey is the planning, and you and your friend can learn a ton and have a wonderful time just plotting your imminent move.

Start by coming up with a place you both want to go. Italy? Kenya? Australia? Japan? A town thirty miles down the road? The possibilities are limitless.

Places I Want to Go: _____

_____

_____

_____

Start researching the place and how you will get there—simply by plane or do you need a boat, train or sled? Investigate the customs and traditions and see if there is a particular time of year when more happens than usual. Research the history of the place and what kind of government it currently has. Make note of all the main sights you should see; look up the touristy ones and the off-the-beaten-path places too. You can also clip any magazine articles or print any Web pages you find on great places to eat or stay.

Hit the library and check out the latest travel guide to your place, and look into language cassettes or CDs if they don't speak the same language as you in your desired destination. Hit up AAA for maps of the place (if your folks are members, they can get them for free). Run through the next week's television listings for the Travel Channel and see if any of the shows are covering your place. If so, mark your calendar or record it for group viewing.

And by all means, look into getting a pen pal in your locale of choice. Ask a teacher at school for a list of safe and legitimate organizations.

If another country feels too far away right now, I urge you to check out the town one over from yours. You can start small and work your way up and out to the rest of the world.

SONG OF THE DAY:
MICHELLE SHOCKED, "ANCHORAGE"
A story-song about one gal in New York and her friend who moves to Anchorage, Alaska, and how the old pals stay in touch via letter writing. Did you know Alaska is the largest state in the Union?

Day TWENTY-EIGHT
FEARLESS FRIENDSHIP

Wonder Twin powers,
Activate! In the form of—
Best friends for all time.

Do you know what frightens your friends most in this world? Do you know what makes them feel stuck in their shoes with fear? It's a weird thing to talk about, and yet if you want to know someone really deep-down well, you probably wanna know what scares 'em.

One of the great joys of friendship is helping someone through their fear. It's not like I'm suggesting that if your pal is scared of spiders you sign her up for *Fear Factor*. I don't think you need to address her fears that directly. I just mean that when you have an understanding of what could ail her, you have a better understanding of her as a person.

Now, I like to think of the opposite of fearful as *adventurous*. It doesn't say so in the dictionary, but the actual definition is not that far off. When we explore our adventurous sides, we become less fearful in general. And when we do this with a friend or two, it becomes not only powerfully life-changing, it also becomes fun and, believe it or not, easier.

When you have a pal by your side it's much easier to feel that bold surge of adrenaline pulsing through your veins. Don't confuse the concept of being adventurous with being stupid or being physically adventurous. Sure, you can go climb mountains together—that would definitely form a unique bond between friends. But I also think you can just be intrepid in your everyday lives. You can face new challenges with gusto; you can be audacious when looking for a new job and cheeky when flirting with the boys. To be adventurous in daily life is to approach it boldly and bravely. By doing that, you and your friends will have deeper connections and will enjoy life more, living it to its fullest.

ACTIVITY 28

You know the movie *The Blair Witch Project*? It was filmed in these long takes with the actors ad-libbing much of what was happening. When they filmed this movie, they used what is called a "safe word" or code word—it was "taco"—when they wanted to break character and talk as actors about how the scene was playing out.

Sometimes when we're out and about and in a conversation with people we don't want to be with, or in a situation we would just love to get out of, we long for a friend to swoop in and save us. But if you and your friends have some sort of code word or words in place, you don't have to just wish they'd come save you from the situation—you can literally call on them. It's a way to ask for help without asking for help.

Your code word can be anything, and the more random it is, the more confusing it will be to the others in the room. They won't know exactly what you're doing and therefore won't be offended. My favorite, though, is far from subtle.

When I was younger, I would say "Wonder Twin powers, activate!" when I wanted out of a jam. My friend Jessica would quickly back me up with " form of—a glacier!" thereby changing the subject, and then she would hastily usher me out of harm's way. It was a bit more than a simple code word, but hey, it worked, and we always giggled plenty afterward.

Are you familiar with Zan and Jayna, the Wonder Twins, who were part of *The All-New Super Friends Hour*? They were from the planet Exor and were able to change form just by holding their rings together and uttering those magic words. Zan usually took on some form of water, while Jayna almost always became an animal.

SONG OF THE DAY:
THE ATARIS, "IN THIS DIARY"
A song about the pleasures of growing up, remembering the past and friendships that meant everything.

DAY TWENTY-NINE
20/20 VISION

I "see" with my eyes,
But "vision" is so much more—
Seeing with eyes closed.

Vision is a quality we look for in leaders, but is it one we need in friends?

Well, you don't need it in every friend and you won't find it in every friend. But when you have great vision you can achieve great things.

Vision isn't one of those things you can see or touch. It's like a combination of intuition and insight mixed with a heaping helping of chutzpah and a whole lot of understanding. It's a tasty soup made up of a variety of characteristics you desire in a friend.

Fact is, you've been honing your own visionary skills

throughout this book. It takes your powers of imagination to envision what you want out of life, where you think it should go, how to get there and who you want to get there with. That's kind of what we've been after these last twenty-eight days. Because when you are the best person you can be, you'll be the best friend you can be, and that will reap you many rewards in the form of one (or maybe even more) fabulous friend giving you that ol' friendship love right back. Which will lead to more understanding, more insight, more vision. It's all a pretty beautiful circle.

ACTIVITY 29

I'm not a huge Fergie fan—she just doesn't float my boat—but I actually got this little idea from an interview with her. So thank you, Fergs.

Grab your pal and check out the little templates on page 159—there is one for you and one for a friend. You can copy them onto a piece of paper or write right here in this book. Note that at the bottom it says "You Are Here." That is you, right now. At the top of the page it says "Big-time Goal" and has a space for you to fill that in. Go ahead, write down your biggest goal—what you want to be, see or accomplish. Now, see the arrows connecting the "You Are Here" to the "Big-time Goal"? I've added a few lines and you're gonna fill them in.

These lines signify the steps it will take you to get from the bottom of the page to the top. So say for instance that you would like to be a fashion designer. Closer to the bottom write down things like "Learn to sew" and "Make my own patterns." But how can you learn those things? Perhaps you could ask an aunt or grandmother who sews, or you could take a class at the local community college. Whatever the options, write them down as well.

Farther up the chart write things such as "Go to design school." And to go to design school you have to apply, so add that in there too. Keep going: add in things like "Sell my clothes on Etsy.com" or "Get my designs into a boutique." And for everything you think of, ask yourself, "What other steps do I need to do to get to that one?" Think of this as a ladder—you're adding the rungs so that you can climb up to your goal. Help each other fill in the blank spaces, the links in the chain all the way up. You'll probably think of things she would forget, and likewise, she'll come up with some stuff you would have left out.

BIG-TIME GOAL: _____

BIG-TIME GOAL: _____

✳ YOU ARE HERE

✳ YOU ARE HERE

And listen, this isn't written in stone; it's written on the page of a book or even a piece of paper you had lying around. While it's sacred in many ways, it's also okay if it changes over time. Add more steps, delete some—you can even change the goal at the top. But keep it available and present for consideration and influence, because you two just made yourselves little plans o' life. Hold each other accountable and encourage each other, as good friends do!

SONG OF THE DAY:
BOB MARLEY, "HIGH TIDE OR LOW TIDE"
We got to have some reggae, mon. Bob Marley, all vision and understanding, gave us this tune about an everlasting friendship. Play this one while you and your friends dream big.

LONG-TERM GOALS

You are my best friend.
The finest way to say that?
I really love you.

You've made it through to the final day of our lessons. I suspect that just by virtue of reading and understanding and doing the things in this book, you are closer to your friends—at least the good ones, the ones worth keeping around—than you were when we started this journey.

Closeness isn't something you can just say you want and then get. And that's why it's here at the *end* of the book, because to gain that closeness you needed to be patient, work toward your goals, learn more about your friends and yourself. Closeness takes time and patience, and yes, some effort, too.

I always get bent when people tell me they fell in love at first sight. It can't be love if it happened just with your eyes. And the same thing can be said for friendship, which, as we have learned, is just another flavor of intimate relationship. You can instantly click with someone, for sure, but to be genuinely close, well, that takes time, energy and elbow grease. It takes trial and it takes error. It takes you opening up to them and them opening up to you, which for some can be a whole lot of painful work. But it's a labor of love.

Closeness doesn't mean two people have to live next door to each other or even in the same town. You can feel truly and genuinely close to a friend who lives halfway around the world. Because it isn't about spatial distance, it's—and this is corny—about a closeness of the heart. It's about really *getting* someone. Thoroughly understanding them and knowing them and still being able to be surprised by them.

One of my best girlfriends, the lovely Miss Keva Marie, and I wrote a book together many years ago. We hung out day in and day out; we knew each other so super-duper well. The good stuff and the stinky stuff too. But one day she offhandedly told me something about her that was shocking (in a good way). I was stunned. I clearly remember screeching to her, "How did I not know this about you after all these years?!" It's those little surprises that make closeness—and great friendships—all the more wonderful and exciting.

ACTIVITY 30

It's time to document our friendships. We do this with photos and mementos and knickknacks and scraps of friendship *stuff*. I recommend making a friendship Matryoshka box for your friend, but your gut instinct may be to keep it all to yourself. Head that feeling off at the pass by creating two—one to hoard and one to pass on as a gift.

What do I mean by a Matryoshka box? You know those Russian dolls that open up to reveal another doll, which opens up to reveal another doll, and so on? Those are Matryoshka dolls! By gathering a bunch of boxes that fit inside one another, you can create the ultimate "scrapbook"—but this one has no real pages.

Now, please, I cannot stress this enough—do not go and spend megabucks at the art supply store on fancy scrapbook supplies. Most of the stuff you want to use can be found at the dollar store, in the recycling bin, at the thrift shop or at a neighborhood garage sale.

You'll need to find at least three, but ideally five, boxes that fit inside one another. This can be tricky. You may have to make smaller boxes out of a bigger box by cutting it down to size and using strong packing tape to secure the sides. Jewelry boxes are perfect; shoe boxes ideal; egg cartons and butter boxes workable.

What else are you going to need? Decorative items like scraps of wrapping paper, fabric, rickrack (that squiggly ribbon trim in Granny's sewing box), magazine clippings, felt, stickers, beads, sequins and more. Anything you can cover the sides with, trim out the corners with, make the whole thing beautiful with. And a *glue stick,* of course.

Then the really important stuff, the stuff of friendship: notes you passed in class, postcards from trips taken and family vacations, school newspaper clippings, party invites, ticket stubs from movies and concerts and theme parks, CD covers from your faves—and yes, photos. Anything that represents the two of you and the good times you have had together.

Start with the smallest box. Cut a piece of paper the same height as the box, but five to ten times longer, and fold it accordion-style so that it fits comfortably inside the box. Glue one end down to the bottom of the box, and then on each of the folded "pages" inscribe meaningful words—things like:

- Lyrics to your favorite songs
- The sayings you overuse with hilarity
- Lists! Her favorite snacks, your silliest moments, your top five crushes and top ten hangouts
- Quotes from your favorite books and movies
- Short stories written in slightly secret code about things you girls have done together
- Her X factor traits from Day Twenty-four
- Any moments of extreme kindness—take this opportunity to say "thank you" in writing.

Decorate the base of the box and the top separately so that they don't have to be unwrapped to be opened. Now go ahead and wrap every box this way.

Nestle the smallest box inside the next smallest and

see how much room you have round the edges. Is it a lot? If so, glue some of those ticket stubs or photos to the inside walls of the box. Coat the top with more photos and mementos. And then place that box inside the next largest and keep going till you have covered every inch of every box with the goods and goodness of your friendship.

Now imagine her face when she opens the first box only to find more and more and more, all about you and her and your best, most wonderful friendship times.

P.S. Of course you can do this all in a traditional photo-album-cum-scrapbook, and that would be rad too.

SONG OF THE DAY:
QUEEN, "YOU'RE MY BEST FRIEND"
This classic seventies anthem is straightforward and gorgeous in that big crazy retro way. Add a mix CD to the friendship boxes and this should end the whole thing on a big, bold, loving note.

Well, you did it. You read the book, you did the activities, and hopefully they've affected your life in major ways. Most of all, I hope you have internalized how very important our girlfriends are to us.

Boys are cute. But even if they are the best gosh-darn boyfriends in the world, they don't replace your girlfriends. Girlfriend-ship has so many different layers that are built on common ground, intuitive communication, shared experiences, sensitive ears and sisterly warmth. Girlfriends are role models; they are inspiration; they are strength. They are love.

And remember, friendship is a thing, but it's also an ongoing process. There is no "The End" like in this here book. It goes on and on and on, changing and morphing and educating and inspiring and delighting. Friendship will continue to give your life kick and love and meaning and happiness. So tackle it with responsibility and respect, and treat it with great lovin' care.

Yours in Friendship,
xo Clea

Clea Hantman

THE ULTIMATE BFF MOVIE MARATHON

Beaches

Clueless

Fried Green Tomatoes

How to Make an American Quilt

Now and Then

Steel Magnolias

Toy Story

The Sisterhood of the Traveling Pants

A League of Their Own

Spice World

Aquamarine

Divine Secrets of the Ya-Ya Sisterhood

MORE SONGS FOR THE ULTIMATE FRIENDSHIP MIX CD

Pink Floyd, "Wish You Were Here"

Wedding Present, "She's My Best Friend"

Oasis, "Acquiesce"

Theme from *Welcome Back, Kotter*

High School Musical cast, "We're All in This Together"

Dido, "Thank You"

Madonna, "I'll Remember"

Gwen Stefani, "Cool"

Michael Jackson, "Ben"

Elton John, "Friends"

Randy Newman (from *Toy Story*), "You've Got a Friend in Me"

Everything but the Girl, "Old Friends"

The Beatles, "With a Little Help from My Friends"

Simon and Garfunkel, "Bridge over Troubled Water"

The Beach Boys, "Friends"

Ben E. King, "Stand by Me"

James Taylor, "You've Got a Friend"

Bill Withers, "Lean on Me"

Katrina and the Waves, "Walking on Sunshine"

Edie Brickell, "Circle of Friends"

Fraggle Rock, "The Friendship Song"

Morrissey, "There's a Place in Hell for Me and My Friends"

Ron Sexsmith, "Best Friends"

. . . and add any of the Songs of the Day!

THE ULTIMATE BFF BOOK CLUB

The Sisterhood of the Traveling Pants by Ann Brashares
The Second Summer of the Sisterhood by Ann Brashares
Girls in Pants by Ann Brashares
Forever in Blue by Ann Brashares
Truth & Beauty by Ann Patchett
Violet & Claire by Francesca Lia Block
Divine Secrets of the Ya-Ya Sisterhood by Rebecca Wells
Charlotte's Web by E. B. White
The Year of Secret Assignments by Jaclyn Moriarty
Circle of Friends by Maeve Binchy
Best Friends by Martha Moody
Stargirl by Jerry Spinelli
Peaches by Jodi Lynn Anderson
Run for Your Life by Marilyn Levy
Winnie-the-Pooh by A. A. Milne
The Friendship Ring series by Rachel Vail
Bass Ackwards and Belly Up by Elizabeth Craft and Sarah Fain
Tattoo by Jennifer Lynn Barnes

THESE SONGS HAVE STRONG MESSAGES ABOUT FRIENDSHIP TROUBLES ENCODED WITHIN.
USE WITH CAUTION.

R.E.M., "All the Right Friends"
Graham Coxon, "Hopeless Friend"
The National, "Friend of Mine"
Big Star, "Thank You Friends"
Maia Hirasawa, "My New Friend"
Nada Surf, "Imaginary Friends"
The Concretes, "New Friend"
Eels, "Ant Farm"

MORE WAYS TO TELL YOUR FRIEND SHE'S THE BEST

- Friendship bracelets—but go beyond. Make friendship pins, friendship necklaces, friendship rings, friendship accessories!

- Apply matching temp tattoos.

- Hit the photo booth together.

- Knit or sew her something. Hit craftster.org for basic tutorials and start crafting for friendship.

- Make her coupons—good for things like "a shoulder to cry on," "a sleepover," "a bitch session" and so on.

- Bake her some cookies for no reason whatsoever, just because.

- Make up a holiday and then make her a card to celebrate it!

- Once it's dark, write her a message in chalk on the sidewalk outside her house. First thing she'll see when she leaves in the morning? Your note!

- Make her a mix CD of all your favorite songs from this book. Or make a CD of your own friendship songs that you've enjoyed together, the ones that mean something to you two.

GREAT GIRLFRIENDS IN HISTORY

Perpetua and Felicitas

Emily Dickinson and Susan H. Gilbert

Susan B. Anthony and Elizabeth Cady Stanton

Lucy and Ethel

Laverne and Shirley

Oprah and Gayle

Mary and Rhoda

Courteney Cox-Arquette and Jennifer Aniston (like their TV
    characters!)

Goldie Hawn and Susan Sarandon

Peppermint Patty and Marcie

Nicole Kidman and Naomi Watts

Drew Barrymore and Cameron Diaz

Betty and Veronica

Ruth and Naomi

Wilma and Betty

THE FIVE *OTHER* FRIENDS EVERY GIRL NEEDS IN HER POSSE

Listen, not every girl can be everything to everyone. Your BFF may rock at secret keeping and she may be exceptional at supporting you in times of need, and hopefully you respect and admire her brainpower. But even if you find the perfect pal to be by your side through good and bad, you still want and need more friends who impact your life in random and lovely ways and who you can dish it all back to. The friend who you have lunch with every once and again, the girl who you can enjoy discussing the latest chick-lit novel or even a classic with, the pal you can go out and kick up your heels with—these are all friends too. They're part of your posse. Treat them as such, but remember, they don't have to be the be-all and end-all in friends.

These are the kinds of friends you want in your pool, be it summer, spring, winter or fall. Or maybe you are one of these types of friends to others. . . .

The Crack-up: This is the person who can bust you up even when you feel low and slow. The gal who always has a witty aside. The person you can do nothing with and still have a remarkably fun time.

The Team Player: This is the girl on your soccer team or who you study with who just knows how to play it even Steven. This is a friend in a group of friends who is always cool, is never snarky and who you just know plays fair.

The Flirt: It's always good to have a solid flirt in your midst. They attract the boys, can teach you of their mysterious ways (or you can watch closely and pick them up for yourself) and are great for wacky weekend fun. Just make sure they know where to draw the (flirting) line!

The Fashion Plate: The stylish girl who always looks stunning and put-together can also help you with your own occasionally misguided fashion sense. She's honest and can tactfully tell you when something doesn't look quite right.

The Guy: Every girl needs at least one guy friend. Guys have unique (male) perspectives on life and love, they come built in with other guy friends, and when they are "just friends," they are so easy to talk to.

CLEA HANTMAN loves her girlfriends. Whether they are old or new, silly or serious, young or getting on in years, they all have a place in her heart. When she's not spending time with her ladies, she keeps busy by writing about what she's learned from them. Clea has written eleven books for young women and has worked in advertising for the likes of Target, Wet Seal, Urban Decay, and Hello Kitty. Every week she delivers advice to the girls at Girlsense.com in her spunky and straightforward Super Clea blog. Clea lives in San Diego with her husband and daughter.